Escaping Normal

Descending
Skies

Marella Sands

Word Posse

Dedication

To Anne Willis, who shares my interest in the weird and unusual,
and who is always up for an adventure to a UFO watchtower or
Mothman Festival or haunted Bed & Breakfast.

The Angels' Share Books

Volume 1: Through a Keyhole, Darkly
Volume 2: What the Thunder Said
Volume 3: The Chair She Sat In
Volume 4: With Sleepless Eye
Volume 5: Past the Isle of Dogs
Volume 6: When We Had Feathers
Volume 7: Feeding the Bird of Tondal
Volume 8: A Heap of Broken Images (coming in 2021)
Volume 9: Her Hair in Fiery Points (coming in 2022)

Other Word Posse Books by Marella Sands

Pandora's Mirror
Fortune's Daughter
Restless Bones

Ring of Fire Press Books by Marella Sands

Perdition
Purgatory
Perfection
Paradise (coming in 2021)
Promised Land (coming in 2022)

Catch up with the author on various platforms:
Facebook: facebook.com/MarellaSands
YouTube: Search *Marella Sands* once there!

ISBN-13: 978-1-944089-46-7

Table of Contents

Introduction

The question is not: "Are UFOs real?" People are definitely seeing something. The question is: "What exactly are they seeing?"
Preston E. Dennett & Rosemary Ellen, Authors of *UFOs and Aliens*

If, as some suggest, people who see UFOs are imagining them or simply seeing things, should this not be cause for some worry, since one in ten people cannot trust their own eyes?
Chris A. Rutkowski, UFO Researcher

***

I saw a UFO once. Well, sort of. In any case, in the late 1980s, a silent black triangle passed over me at a low altitude. I instantly realized I was seeing exactly the sort of thing people report as UFOs. I mean, there it was. All big and black and silent!

However, I lived near an airport and was used to airplanes flying over at a similar altitude. While I couldn't explain why any airplane flying so low over my head should be *silent*, I chalked it up to some atmospheric weirdness.

As the object passed overhead, it banked to the right to line up with a runway. Once it banked, I could clearly see the fuselage of the aircraft. I still couldn't hear it, but the experience did give me an object lesson on how easily our senses can be fooled. The craft was not actually black, nor was it triangular, and, whether I could hear it or not, it was not silent. Because, you know, planes just *aren't*.

I also saw Bigfoot tracks once. That was in 1977, when I was in fifth grade. In the early morning, I spotted bare footprints in the snow across our playground at the elementary school I attended. Fortunately, we were doing a photography lab in my class, and so I had a camera on me. I took four pictures of the prints and so I can, assuming I can find them, demonstrate that someone, or some creature, walked through the snow barefoot on that winter's day decades ago.

And then there was the time I saw a ghost. I was very small, maybe three years old, and, looking back on it now, I'm pretty sure what I saw was the flash of headlights running along the wall of my bedroom. The important thing for me at the time was that I was scared out of my mind. What I remember most about that incident, though, is that no one believed me, and that made me very angry. I wonder if that incident has been the reason I have a difficult, if not impossible, time watching a movie or television show where someone is telling the truth and no one believes them. As soon as that plot develops, I stop watching.

Perhaps my experience was undergirded by the recurring Sesame Street skit where Big Bird saw the Snuffleupagus and no one believed him, either. I know Snuffy is seen by everyone now, but in the early 1970s, he was assumed by everyone—except Big Bird and the audience—to be a figment of Big Bird's imagination. This made me outraged on Big Bird's behalf, because I could clearly see he wasn't lying!

Yes, I suppose I need therapy. Because of ghost stories. And Sesame Street.

Anyway...

As soon as I learned to read, I quickly became a consumer of books documenting the strange, bizarre, and wonderful. I grew up on John Keel, Erich von Däniken, D. Scott Rogo, Harry Price, and any book of the unusual labeled "true stories." My favorite book was one of ghost stories that I checked out of the library several times a year. I wish I could remember the title because I'd love to have a copy now! (Oh well...)

The more books I read, the more books I wanted to read. The subject could be ghosts, ancient aliens, poltergeists, fairies, crystal skulls, alien abductions, Atlantis, hollow earth, the Nazca lines, or any of a hundred other things. I read them all. I read them multiple times. I just *read*.

I never found the books convincing in terms of believing aliens were actually visiting our planet, or that ghosts and poltergeists truly existed in the world around me. Yet I still went on ghost tours, stayed in haunted locations, and put ghost hunting characters in my fiction works. In fact, I have had enough ghosts and ghost hunting in my books and short stories that people have told me I should start ghost hunting myself, "since you clearly love the subject so much."

I've bought books on ghost hunting, but no, I have not yet become a ghost hunter. Maybe someday, when I have time for another hobby! In the meantime, I look forward to staying in more haunted hotels and participating in more ghost tours, to go looking for spook lights and seeking out the Mothman of Point Pleasant. I will continue to read up on the latest UFO flaps and watch YouTube videos that claim to have captured paranormal events. *Because I love this stuff!* Honestly, who doesn't love a good mystery, especially if it comes complete with an otherworldly story attached?

This series came about because, not only do I love these subjects, but because I know there are many people out there who'd like to share their stories, and I want to hear them. I may not now believe, nor may ever believe, in the objective reality of the paranormal events in the stories. But I am willing to believe those who experience these things have actually experienced *something*. Because I believe the vast majority of people who experience something are telling the truth. And telling the truth while not being believed is, well, frustrating, to be nice about it. I get it.

Who knows, by the end of the series, perhaps I'll be a believer. Anything's possible. And if not, at least I will have delved even further into the fascinating world of the odd and unexplainable.

I hope you have as much fun reading these books as I am having researching and writing them.

Looking to the Skies

As I looked, behold, a stormy wind came out of the north, and a great cloud, with brightness around it, and fire flashing forth continually, and in the midst of the fire, as it were gleaming metal. As for the appearance of the wheels and their construction: their appearance was like the gleaming of beryl. And the four had the same likeness, their appearance and construction being as it were a wheel within a wheel. When they went, they went in any of the four directions without turning. Their rims were tall and awesome, and the rims of all four were full of eyes all around.
Ezekiel 1:4,16-18

The Pushpaka chariot that resembles the Sun and belongs to my brother was brought by the powerful Ravana; it resembled a bright cloud in the sky, and the King got in, and it rose up into the higher atmosphere.
Ramayana

✻
✻✻

Flying ships aren't a new thing. They appeared to prophets in the Old Testament, to the characters of Indian sagas, to pharaohs and Roman armies. Not having the vocabulary to discuss extraterrestrials and their air/spacecraft, people chalked these visions up to being from the gods, or even being gods themselves, although the Roman authors, at least, were a bit more prosaic than that.

One of the first examples someone familiar with the Bible is likely to come up with is the wheels which Ezekiel saw, which were clearly both impressive and, let's face it, deeply disturbing. If you can read *the rims...were full of eyes all around* and not be creeped out, or even flat-out terrified, you're a better person than me.

But the Bible is not the only source for such tales, as the quote from the Ramayana makes plain. Interestingly, some modern translators like to take the word here glossed as *chariot* as turn it into *car* or *aircraft*, in order to make the connection to possible alien visitation more obvious. I'm not sure such a translation is required; any chariot that takes people "into the higher atmosphere" must surely be divine, or at the very least, a technological wonder unknown to the person describing the event.

Livy discussed ships in the sky in 218 B.C.E., while Pliny the Elder wrote about "sparks" ascending into heaven over the Roman Republic in 76 B.C.E. Plutarch recorded that silver wine jar-shaped objects fell over a battlefield in 74 B.C.E. and Cassius Dio penned a passage about fine silver filaments falling from a clear sky in 196 C.E. It is worthwhile to note that only Cassius Dio was a contemporary of the actual event, though whether he witnessed the filaments falling, or only heard the story later from others, I do not know. The others were reporting on matters that had happened many years, even centuries, before they were born. Therefore, the odds that those events were merely tall tales, or had at least been significantly embellished, are pretty good, sadly. After all, everybody knows what happens over time to the size of the fish the fisherman *almost* caught.

Interestingly, the Roman authors do not seem much concerned with attaching these stories to particular gods. They simply describe what the eyewitnesses claimed to have seen, apparently without feeling the need to ponder the nature of such things or the origins of them. Silver jars fell, filaments covered the ground, and sparks rose into the atmosphere. Story reported. There you go.

It may not be too much of a stretch to turn to myths of ancient cultures to look for evidence of odd things in the sky and wonder what the story might *really* be about. A UFO encounter could be bundled into local legends of dragons or sun chariots or any number of other storied creatures or things that, today, do not strike us as being remotely like a UFO at all. It is all well and good that Aquila the Eagle was sent by Zeus to kidnap the young shepherd Ganymede, but we could certainly posit that, if a UFO appeared and a shepherd ended up being taken away, never to be seen again, Zeus would probably have been a good deity to blame for such a thing. In fact, considering Zeus' propensity for kidnapping and/or raping defenseless humans, it is not such a leap to wonder if both the phenomenon of UFOs and that of alien abductions could be laid at his door.

I mean, Zeus wasn't exactly a nice guy to, well, anyone, especially anyone who caught his fancy. But that is largely the way ancient gods were: jealous, angry, and given to brutalizing poor humans. The god of the Old Testament and those in the Ramayana are no exceptions. It's not hard to see why: life was, as it has been put by Thomas Hobbes, nasty, brutish, and short, and if that's what humans were demonstrably like to other humans every day, why would the gods be any better? The ancients do not seem to have thought that their gods could, or should, be held any more to account than their fellow

Rapt de Ganymede, J. Briot, 17th Century. (Wikimedia Commons)

humans, which is either very practical, or very sad. Or both.

In any case, by the middle ages, people were once again noticing things in the sky, and bothering to write them down. Because, you know, we're not going to know of any incident that someone saw that they did not then either write down or have someone else write down. The incident, and memory of it, would have died with them and the few people to whom they told their tale.

So who knows what stories have been lost over time due to a lack of literacy? Probably a lot.

In any case, an entire aerial battle was observed by the citizens of Nuremberg back in 1561 C.E. The flying machines engaging in the battle apparently included ships shaped like cylinders and spheres, and even a large black triangular object was noted at one point. Many of these objects then crashed to the ground outside of the city.

A translation of the report of this battle is given as follows. The globes and arcs and rods have appeared in the sky and then:

These all started to fight among themselves, so that the globes, which were first in the sun, flew out to the ones standing on both sides, thereafter, the globes standing outside the sun, in the small and large rods, flew into the sun. Besides the globes flew back and forth among themselves and fought vehemently with each other for over an hour. And when the conflict in and again out of the sun was most intense, they became fatigued to such an extent that they all, as said above, fell from the sun down upon the earth 'as if they all burned' and they then wasted away on the earth with immense smoke. After all this there was something like a black spear, very long and thick, sighted; the shaft pointed to the east, the point pointed west. Whatever such signs mean, God alone knows.

The Celestial Phenomenon over Nuremberg by Hanns Glaser, 1561. (Wikimedia Commons)

Now that is an eyewitness account to end all eyewitness accounts! Flying rods and globes fighting with each other, becoming fatigued, and crashing to the ground, only to "waste away with immense smoke." That had to be a sight to behold. As you can see, the incident was recorded for posterity in art. It depicts quite the scene.

But Nuremberg was not the only place in Europe where odd objects in the sky were observed. Just five years later, in 1566, a bunch of spheres appeared in the skies over Basel, Switzerland, and a century later, in 1668, a *silver lizard*, of all things, was observed over Levoča in what is now Slovakia.

Other countries were not immune. In 1803, fishermen in Japan reported a strange red-and-white haired woman in an odd vessel who, while speaking a language they had never previously heard, still managed to communicate to them that the box she held was not to be touched by them. Which, if you think about it, is a really odd story. Why bother to land your craft on the ocean just to tell some guys in a fishing boat *This is my box. You can't touch it?* Especially since you're not speaking their language and so have to figure out how to communicate this idea somehow via...telepathy? Sign language? Who knows?

Newspapers in New Zealand reported strange lights in the sky in 1909, and, famously, World War II fighter pilots reported metallic spheres and odd balls of light in both theaters of war. These were the "foo fighters" whose designation might have sunk into complete obscurity except that, in 1994, a rock group decided it would make a good band name.

By the end of World War II, things seemed to be heating up with the odd occurrences in the sky. During 1946, odd lights had been seen overhead in Scandinavia, as well as over many places in the United States. No one knew what to do, though during the so-called Battle of Los Angeles in 1942, military personnel were more than happy to fire thousands of anti-aircraft rounds at whatever they thought they saw over the city.

Then came 1947, and everything changed.

The Modern Age

The intelligence office of the 509th Bombardment Group at Roswell Army Air Field announced at noon today, that the field has come into the possession of a Flying Saucer.
Roswell Daily Record, 8 July 1947

These objects more or less fluttered like they were, oh, I'd say, boats on very rough water or very rough air of some type, and when I described how they flew, I said that they flew like they take a saucer and throw it across the water. Most of the newspapers misunderstood and misquoted that too. They said that I said that they were saucer-like; I said that they flew in a saucer-like fashion.
Kenneth Arnold
Interviewed by Edward R. Murrow, 1950

*
**

Here's the good news: the dog does not die in this story. Actually, there was never, apparently, a dog at all.

But it's cool that the story has a dog. It also has a UFO, weird slaglike detritus, and Men in Black. As the story goes, in June 1947, two men, Fred L. Crisman and Harold Dahl, along with Dahl's dog, were out in Puget Sound when a UFO came by and dropped some slag in the Sound. One piece struck the dog, which was killed. The UFO then flew off. Less than twenty-four hours later, Crisman and Dahl were approached by some odd Men in Black suits who threatened them.

> **Fun Fact**
> I know that the new term is UAP (Unidentified Aerial Phenomena) but I'll be sticking with the tried-and-true term UFO for this book.

It all makes for a pretty exciting story, with everything from UFOs polluting Earth's waterways, to a murdered pet, to threats to civilian lives by nameless men from unknown agencies. Even today, the story lives on as The Maury Island Incident, and I have heard it recounted in various YouTube videos as a well-documented and believable story. The tale has legs, and just keeps on going.

However, Crisman confessed later that the entire thing was made up. Exactly why he and Dahl made it up is a little more difficult to explain, but apparently Crisman was known to confabulate incidents for his own...amusement, I guess? Which at least was good news for the dog.

But 1947 didn't just see the fictional Maury Island account. That was the year flying saucers *really* took off.

Flying Saucers

Anyone reading this book has, no doubt, heard of Kenneth Arnold and the infamous account which actually gave rise to the term *flying saucer*. But I recount it here in brief because it is so important to everything that came after.

So, to sum up: Kenneth Arnold was flying near Mt. Rainier, Washington, when he spotted nine flying objects. He first wondered if they were geese but quickly realized the objects were metallic in nature and flying far too quickly to be birds. Arnold then assumed these were some kind of new military jet, but oddly, he noted they were not shaped like jets. He described one as "crescent-shaped" and the other eight as "convex-shaped." They "skipped" through the atmosphere and wove from side to side. They were far more maneuverable than any Earth aircraft, though at the time, Arnold still believed he was looking at experimental aircraft from the U.S. military.

Arnold watched the objects for some time and, after doing some calculations, decided the nine craft were moving at approximately 1700mph (2700kph). This was clearly far too fast for any U.S. military jet, experimental or not, which gave Arnold some pause.

After landing, Arnold excitedly told others what he had seen, but was not believed. Later, he told some former Army pilots about the incident, and they informed him that they had been briefed about foo fighters during the war. Therefore, they were confident that he had seen *something*, though what that something was exactly, they did not know. Still, they assured Arnold that strange objects had been seen by pilots before, and that he was not crazy.

However, the story then began to take on a life of its own. Within three days, Arnold was complaining that he hadn't had "a moment of peace" since he'd shared the story and that he'd even been informed by a pastor that these objects were a sign of the end times. A woman in a café allegedly ran from the establishment screaming that here was the man who had seen "men from Mars."

Arnold later conducted his own investigation as to the nature of the objects. It did not take long for him to conclude that they were craft made of a material "unknown to the civilization of this earth."

Flying saucers were now, more or less, officially extraterrestrial in nature.

Roswell, New Mexico

The other elephant in the room when there's any discussion of UFOs is, of course, Roswell.

Again, a brief summary: in July 1947, something came down in a field near Roswell, New Mexico. A local foreman working on a ranch noticed debris and, though initially uninterested, he eventually returned with his wife and son, and the three of them began collecting the bits of metal and rubber that they found. Eventually, this came to the attention of the local sheriff, who theorized the debris might have come from a "flying disc." Eventually, staff from the local Army Air Field came to see the pieces and retrieve them.

At first, there seemed to be no real mystery. Despite the sheriff's imaginative interpretation, the military, as well as most of the civilians who had any knowledge of the incident, were confident the item was a crashed weather balloon. In fact, some of the pieces retrieved had *Scotch tape* on them!

A press release was issued from the military stating that the object had been a weather balloon and, for thirty years, no one thought another thing about it.

However, by the 1970s, when interest in UFOs began to increase substantially, the conspiracy theorists began to come out of the woodwork. More and more Americans were admitting to pollsters that they believed aliens existed and had visited Earth. As time went on and conspiracy theories took even greater hold of the public imagination, more people revealed they now believed that it had been an alien craft that had crashed at Roswell, and not a weather balloon at all.

Between the books, TV show, and videos, Roswell has become a phenomenon all on its own. The town has embraced its calling as a center of UFO interest and is now the site of the International UFO Museum and Research Center. I do intend to get there one day.

To 1948...And Beyond
Things did not slow down after 1947, though subsequent UFO sightings have not risen to the levels of awareness in the general population that the Arnold and Roswell incidents had. Whereas most people today probably have at least heard of Roswell, most do not know the later sightings or have only heard vague things about them.

An alleged UFO sighted over Passaic, New Jersey, in 1952. (Wikimedia Commons)

In any case, incidents after 1947 increased so much, no one could keep up with them all. Up to now, UFOs had been hoaxes, weather balloons, or the something-we-don't-know-what-it-was Kenneth Arnold saw. But things were about to get deadly.

In Alabama, a UFO was reported to "nearly" have collided with an airplane, which was bad enough, but a UFO sighting over Fort Knox, Kentucky, in January of 1948 resulted in the death of the pilot of the craft tasked with following the UFO.

A "ball of light" engaged in a cat-and-mouse chase with a pilot in a P-51 Mustang over Fargo, North Dakota in October of the same year.

Throughout the 1950s, more lights and flying saucers were spotted over multiple states, including Oregon, Montana, Texas, Virginia, Nevada, West Virginia, South Dakota, and North Dakota. International incidents were documented in Brazil, South Africa, Italy, Canada, Japan, France, the Soviet Union, Australia, the United Kingdom, Iran, Poland, New Zealand, Peru, Spain, Belgium, Mexico, and Finland. And I'm sure that's not the complete list.

Soon, a new phenomenon became recognized. Once a UFO was reported in an area, other people began coming forward to give their stories as well. Whether or not these people were seeing the same thing as the original person who reported the incident, or whether they simply couldn't stand to be left out of whatever exciting thing was going on in their neighborhood, I do not know. However, these clumps of sightings soon became referred to as "flaps."

In 1952, a UFO flap occurred over Washington, D.C. Strange objects were seen that reportedly flew faster than the jets sent to intercept them. Civilian and military pilots gave eyewitness testimony to the odd things they'd seen in the skies over D.C. An air traffic controller saw so many blips on his screen he joked about seeing a "fleet of flying saucers." The Air Force had to form a special unit to investigate the sheer volume of cases. Sightings were reported to many major newspapers and given headlines like "Jets Chase D.C. Sky Ghosts" and "Saucers Swarm Over Capital."

The jokes died when the objects began flying over the White House and the Capitol building. More jets were sent on more intercepts. One pilot reported, "I saw several bright lights. I was at maximum speed, but even then I had no closing speed. I ceased chasing them because I saw no chance of overtaking them." This being the Cold War, people worried these might be secret technology from the Soviet Union. Perhaps they were even nuclear weapons of some kind.

That became known as "the Big Flap."

By this time, the circumstances around these flaps began to show that people were forming their own vocabulary around these incidents. As people encountered the unusual in the sky, and increasingly, on the ground, they needed a way to speak about the encounters that helped convey what people felt was going on.

The movie *Close Encounters of the Third Kind*, sometimes abbreviated as *CE3K*, introduced many people to the idea that there were "kinds" of close encounters with extraterrestrials. The original list of "kinds" was drawn up by J. Allen Hynek. Hynek, the director of Ohio State University's McMillin Observatory, had a high security clearance due to his work with the government during World War II, and so he may have seemed like the obvious go-to when the Air Force needed someone to help them sort out just what was going on in the skies.

Hynek recalled that he was originally approached by men who were clearly embarrassed by the reason for their visit, though ultimately they were able to force themselves to ask him about flying saucers and whether or not Hynek might want to consult on the matter with the Air Force. Hynek said later, "The job didn't seem as though it would take too much time, so I agreed." That agreement would change the course of his life. "I had scarcely heard of UFOs in 1948 and, like every other scientists I knew, assumed that they were nonsense."

With a cynical eye, Hynek spent the next year consulting with the Air Force on the rather boringly named *Project Sign*, and ended up classifying the Air Force's data into several types: astronomical phenomena (32% of sightings); other identifiable objects such as flares, birds, or balloons (35% of sightings); unclassifiable due to lack of information (13% of sightings); and unexplained (20% of sightings). Though fully 20% of the sightings were still labeled *unidentified*, the Air Force felt justified in reporting that UFOs did not represent a threat to national security, and that they were merely a combination of hoaxes, hysteria, mental illness, or misinterpretations of terrestrial items like balloons. The Air Force, clearly, was willing to write everything off.

However, the flaps continued, no matter how desperate the military was for them to stop. With no less a personage than Edward R. Murrow delving into the phenomenon, and *Life* magazine running stories on it, the UFO had entered the mainstream, and was here to stay. The Air Force wasn't going to be able to wave away the interest. So in 1952, they asked Hynek to return for their next dive into explaining away sightings: *Project Blue Book.*

Project Blue Book

Project Blue Book was active from 1952 to 1969. As before, Hynek spent a lot of his time reading reports. But he was now given the chance, at least once in a while, to get out into the field where he could observe the location of the sighting and interview the people involved.

Hynek quickly discovered that the people who were making the sightings, people who had merely been names on Air Force reports in the past, suddenly came into focus for him. These were not, for the most part, crackpots, crazy people, or people with some kind of mental deficiency. Words like *hysteria, hallucinations, mental illness,* or *hoax* didn't match up with what he was seeing in the field. Sure, a few people might be lying, and a few might have some issues that made them more likely than others to imagine a sighting. But most people were not like that. "Their standing in the community, their lack of motive for perpetration of a hoax, their own puzzlement at the turn of events they believed they witnessed, and often their great reluctance to speak of the experience," lent the witnesses credibility that no bare bones paper report could replicate.

In fact, much like Kenneth Arnold had discovered in 1947, going public with a story of witnessing UFOs could have more

> **Fun Fact**
> By the time it was shuttered, Project Blue Book had investigated 12,618 cases.

negative repercussions than positive. Some witnesses ended up divorced. Others found that their children were being harassed. People's houses were violated. Their neighbors pulled away, as if there were something contagious about claiming to have seen something unidentified in the sky. The high social, and personal, costs some people paid for going public made Hynek reluctant to be too cynical. He decried the ridicule and ostracizing some people experienced and spoke out against it. Not only did it harm the people involved, but it meant that others, seeing the cost, did not come forward, and any other sightings, or data that might be gleaned from a sighting, were lost to research.

Hynek angered both the military (one Air Force Major considered him a "liability") and believers (the time he theorized about swamp gas, he was derided). But he stayed with Project Blue Book until the end.

Unfortunately, his opinions of those involved with the project was that the staff was inadequate, their communication with scientists was horrible, and their statistical methods "a travesty."

Toward the end of the 1960s, the Air Force, under some pressure from Congress to involve more civilians, organized a committee to study the phenomenon of UFOs. Hynek was not invited to be on it. Two years later, when the committee gave their report, which has become known as the Condon Report, after the chair of the committee, Dr. Edward U. Condon, they recommended that further study of UFOs could not be justified.

Hynek's opinion of the report was that it was "poorly organized" and "slanted." However, his opinion carried no weight. Within a year, Project Blue Book was shut down.

Close Encounters

Hynek's involvement with the Air Force might have ended, but his involvement with UFOs had not. He began writing books about the phenomenon. It was in his 1972 book, *The UFO Experience*, that Hynek first published his classifications of "kinds" of UFO contact.

The first three classifications have become less well-known than the second three, but Hynek's categories were:

1. Nocturnal Lights;
2. Daylight Disks;
3. Radar-Visual (UFOs spotted by both, not just one or the other);
4. Close Encounter of the First Kind: close enough to see details;
5. Close Encounter of the Second Kind: physical evidence such as landing marks or scorched plant material;
6. Close Encounter of the Third Kind: seeing the aliens yourself.

This last category, of course, was used as the title of the movie. It has since been broken down in to sub-categories by subsequent researchers, and other categories have been added.

1. Close Encounter of the Third Kind:
   a. observing an alien inside its craft;

b. observing an alien inside and outside its craft;
c. observing an entity near a craft, but it is not observed exiting or entering the vehicle;
d. observing an entity; no craft is visible, but there have been reports of UFOs in the area;
e. observing an entity but no craft is visible and no UFO activity has been reported;
f. no entity or craft are observed but the witness experiences some kind of communication that seems to them to be from an intelligence.

2. Close Encounter of the Fourth Kind: abduction and, generally, experimentation upon humans by the entity or entities;
3. Close Encounter of the Fifth Kind: communication and contact, but in this case, cooperative contact, with the entity or entities;
4. Close Encounter of the Sixth Kind: this involves the death(s) of animals and/or humans, such as cattle mutilations;
5. Close Encounter of the Seventh Kind: hybridization of humans with the entities. (*My appreciation goes out to Loren Petrich, who collated these onto a single web page, which meant I didn't have to go searching all over the web for them.*)

Spielberg's movie only whetted the public appetite for more. As more people became aware of the different "kinds" of contact, and more reports came in, Hollywood continued to notice. Between the release of *Close Encounters of the Third Kind* and the turn of the century, TV shows such as 3rd *Rock From the Sun, ALF, Alien Nation, Code Name: Eternity, Hard Time on Planet Earth, The Phoenix, The Powers of Matthew Star, Starman, Something Is Out There, Dark Skies, Earth: Final Conflict, First Wave, Invasion: Earth,* and *War of the Worlds* featured aliens either living on, or invading, Earth. Another series, *Project U.F.O.,* even dramatized the investigations of Project Blue Book.

Aliens had certainly been featured before, but now they were everywhere. And their popularity hadn't even begun to waver.

Personal Story: Lauretta Allen

So, another time, him [my father] and my mom had gone fishing and they were out on the boat. My dad liked to go out before the sun came up so they were out there at like 5:00 a.m. This would have been early 70s, I guess. And he and her both had the same story for this, which always lends more credence to it whenever both people see the same thing. So, this red light came down and hovered over the lake. And then it did the whole zip-zip-zip going in all these weird different directions. By this point my mother is freaking out. And my dad was like, "What in the hell is that?" And then it hovered again and then it just went "zoom" and took off.

My dad always saw weird things. He saw ball lightning, he saw a fair weather tornado, he saw the spout, the water tornado thing. He said the ball lightning was the coolest thing he'd ever seen. Well, he'd seen all that stuff so he was like, "no, it wasn't ball lightning," it wasn't this, it wasn't that. He was just like, it was obviously something, he thought, something not normal.

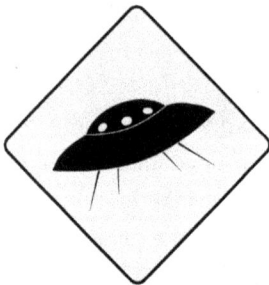

UFO Warning Sign by Cybergedeon (Wikimedia Commons)

The only other one I remember him telling me was on the night that his brother was buried so this was 1967. So grandma's house was about a half a mile, maybe a quarter mile, from the church and it was out in the country. It was this little white picket church, you know?

And they had his funeral and buried him and later that night they were all sitting out in the front yard talking, and they said you could see this huge white glowing light coming up from where the church was. And they were all going to get in the car to drive up there to see what was going on, when this car came speeding down the road and pulls into my grandma's driveway and it was the preacher who'd done the funeral. And he had been at the church. And my dad said he almost fell getting out of the car. He was like, "Oh, my god. There was a big bright white light hovering over the cemetery." The whole cemetery, not just my uncle, but the whole cemetery. My grandmother had to give him a shot of whiskey because he was shaking so bad. So, yeah, that's all the alien stories.

New Century, New Tech

While most sightings have conventional explanations, I think it is stunning how many reports come in regularly to groups like MUFON, with impressive detail, including photos or videos. I often hear from skeptics, "If UFOs are out there how come nobody ever gets a video with all the smartphones around?" That is ignorant—it happens all the time.
Chris Mellon, former Deputy Assistant Secretary of Defense for Intelligence

Whether we ever get to know about them or not, there are very probably alien civilizations that are superhuman, to the point of being god-like in ways that exceed anything a theologian could possibly imagine. Their technical achievements would seem as supernatural to us as ours would seem to a Dark Age peasant transported to the twenty-first century. Imagine his response to a laptop computer, a mobile telephone, a hydrogen bomb, or a jumbo jet.
Richard Dawkins, Evolutionary Biologist and Author

***

There's a meme going around that strikes me as funny. In the top half, it shows a 1960s-era housewife talking on the phone saying, "I can't say that or the government will wiretap my phone." In the bottom half, a woman speaks to her Alexa and says, "Wiretap—I need a recipe for pot roast."

We saw similar concerns in 2020 with conspiracy theorists simultaneously worried about Bill Gates using coronavirus vaccines to inject microchips into their bodies which would aid the government in tracking them, *while carrying tracking devices in their pockets.*

Times, as they say, have changed. And yet, they have not. The conspiracy theorists remain; they just alter their theory a bit here and there, and not always in ways that make sense. After all, why *would* Bill Gates want to microchip everyone, especially since people are already paying Apple for a tracking device that they then carry around on them at all times?

Try to find out information about yourself online. Where do you live? What is your favorite restaurant? Where did you go to high school? No doubt a few Google searches will be all it takes to acquire that information. We have fully entered the information age, but we haven't yet entirely caught up on what that means.

The Tracking Device in Your Pocket
Though I resisted at first, it turns out I'm just as much a cell phone junkie as the next person. I think my initial reluctance to get one was that I don't really want a *phone* in my pocket. I don't make that many calls.

But I do use e-mail a lot. I am old enough that I now require a shopping list instead of relying on my memory to get me through the grocery store without forgetting half my items. I am now used to being able to play Solitaire when I'm bored, looking up what's new at the Red Box whenever I'm out, checking the opening hours of a business that's down the street, getting directions to a location I've never visited before, or reading the menu of the new restaurant in town. I take pictures of my pets, check my UPS deliveries, and track my Amazon packages. I do all of this on a device I refer to as my *phone* but which is almost never used for actual phone calls.

The very first time my husband looked up something on the internet on his phone, we were at a restaurant. The rest of us were astonished. He looked up something on the internet *on his phone! In a restaurant!* He might as well have done magic.

These days, I'm annoyed if I can't get to the internet *immediately*, no matter where I am, and no matter what reason I think I need it for.

My life is significantly different than it was just over ten years ago. Cell phones are a major reason why. Without knowing you, I'm pretty sure your life is different, too.

Having this marvel of technology on me at all times has resulted in some wrinkles in my life I hadn't even *thought of* as wrinkles. Do I want to text

> **Fun Fact**
> Statistica.com estimates that the number of smartphone users will top 3.8 billion in 2021. That's a lot of tracking devices!

someone I'm going to be late? No problem. Do I want to get the same brand of pasta as last time? I can take a picture of the bar code from inside the grocery store's app and I'll even know if they currently have that brand and type of pasta in stock.

Magic is all around.

Beyond the phone is the world wide web, which is the magical thing that makes the smartphone "smart." It's what allows me to order my DoorDash and track its progress to my home, look up statistics for this book, and communicate with my students via Zoom (at least, as long as we're still not meeting in person).

And that has meant a sea-change for the UFO experiencer and researcher alike.

When Dr. Hynek got reports from the Air Force, they were no doubt typed on a typewriter. At best, they were replicated on a mimeograph machine. Interviews had to be conducted in person or over the phone. If they were recorded, the recording device was unwieldy, recorded data onto a magnetic tape, and probably had poor performance in the field (not to mention having to be plugged in to an outlet).

Today's researcher can forget all that. Multiple platforms are available to perform interviews online. Smartphones can record video as well as audio, and have batteries which can last for hours in the field. The GPS app on the phone can be used to track one's own movements (my husband has used this to show the route of our hikes). The internet itself can be used to store huge amounts of data, such as databases which can be designed for anyone in the world with internet services to access for certain functions.

With all this technology available, it is no wonder than UFO sightings can now be reported almost in real-time, and the internet hosts databases that encourage you to submit your UFO sighting information. According to the site ufostalker.com, there were 5262 sightings (an average of 14 per day) reported to their database in 2020. February 2021 had 245 (an average of 8 per day).

As I am looking at their database right now, I can see that the most recent sighting was yesterday over Ball Ground, Georgia. When I click on the entry, I am shown a case number, the date of the occurrence, the date of the report, the source, the location (down to the ZIP code), the duration of the incident, the flight path of the object, and its shape. In this case, I can see that the object was cylindrical, was bright white, traveled in a straight line at treetop height, was viewed for twenty seconds, and the person reporting the incident was not able to take a photo or video of it (though it appears, from their comments, that they did try). The person estimated it was no more than 100 feet from them when they observed it.

Consider this database has over 100,000 entries. Though I do not know the date of the oldest entry, that is certainly a lot of data! The website also includes a gallery of images submitted, no doubt, from users, and discussion forums where people can talk about what they saw.

This is the sort of data and ability to connect with thousands of observers and experiencers that Hynek could only have dreamed about.

Technology Today, Technology Tomorrow
What's next for technology and UFOs? We can already take photos and video with devices in our pockets, upload the photos and video to a world wide web from almost anywhere in the world to almost anyone on the planet almost instantaneously. We can post in forums, petition the government, start blogs, make YouTube videos, and communicate via Zoom or other platforms at our leisure.

What could possibly be next?

Several years ago, I read an article about contact lenses that would be able to track your blood sugar and, though wi-fi, upload the data to your doctor's office. Other articles have discussed how much we might be able to do with such contact lenses besides upload health information to the web.

Some UFO researchers believe some of this tech, from the chemical composition of new materials, to the construction of aircraft such as the

SR-72 Blackbird and the B-2 stealth bomber are reverse-engineered from objects which fell from the skies.

Direct links are alleged to have been drawn between modern military drones and a UFO crash in Pennsylvania in December 1965. Local authorities supposedly found the military at the crash site by the time they arrived. Though a meteor was fingered as the thing which fell to earth, some researchers claim that eyewitnesses saw a metallic craft, which changed direction several times, and which crashed more-or-less intact. It was this nearly-intact craft which the military showed an interest in.

Interestingly, eyewitnesses apparently saw some kind of alien glyphs on the craft, and tried to copy them down before the military removed the craft from the crash site. These glyphs have now allegedly shown up on secret military aircraft that UFO researchers claim to have pictures of.

Other military drones have been photographed which do not appear to have propulsion systems. UFO researchers posit these craft have been constructed with alien technology which permit the craft to fly in ways the rest of us do not currently understand.

The military areas which have been identified by UFO researchers as the places in which reverse engineering is happening are Area 51 in and Dulce Base, both of which are in New Mexico. Additionally, the down of Dulce is theorized to be undermined by many tunnels which are also areas where reverse-engineering of alien technology is happening.

However, not even the UFO researchers claim to have a great deal of evidence of reverse-engineering being used in our modern technology. In fact, one idea is that these images they have are, yes, hoaxes, but military hoaxes put out there to distract the UFO researchers and to keep them from uncovering even greater secrets. The more researchers chase their tails on well-crafted doctored photos, the less likely they are to discover what the military is *really* doing.

That, at least, seems like a somewhat plausible theory, though it doesn't actually follow that whatever secrets the military is keeping are related to alien technology.

In the end, the technology in your pocket and in things like the B-2 stealth bomber or the International Space Station are wonders, definitely.

But reverse-engineered? That is something which, while theorized, cannot be confidently put forth as something that has actually happened.

The Age of the Atom

*To begin with, many aspects of UFO sightings have to do with the
paranormal; yet psychic phenomena, paranormal phenomena have been
consistently pushed under the rug by most UFO investigators. That is due
in part to the fact that witnesses tell you such things only after you have
gained their trust. But very often they are a challenge to the beliefs or the
world view of the investigators. They may not be ready to hear it or they
may not publish it because they think it would damage their credibility.
And since they are in the business of giving credibility to the subject they
don't want to reveal the paranormal aspects of it.*
Jacques Vallee, UFOlogist and Author

*The Air Force is lying about the national security implications of aerial
objects at nuclear bases.*
Robert Salas, Author of *Unidentified: The UFO Phenomenon*

*\
**

The Mushroom Cloud Over Humankind
More than likely, everyone who reads this sentence knows about nuclear
weapons and can name the only two times they have been used against
other people. What you may not know, reader, is that UFOs have shown
a decided interest in our nuclear capabilities, and have since Day One.

The military began to take UFOs seriously in 1947, when three
months of UFO sightings had the military in a bit of a pickle. Sure,
sightings could just be cases of mistaken identity, but there were *so many*.
The military is supposed to be in the business of protecting the nation,
but protect it from what, exactly? Nobody knew. The Pentagon called for

an investigation, and Air Force Lt. General Nathan F. Twining was put on the case.

Originally dubbed Secret, the documents from Twining's investigation have since been published. They show that, in the opinions of Twining and his team members,

- UFOs were real in the sense that people were seeing *something*. Sightings weren't, for the most part, hallucinations or lies.
- Sometimes, sightings were the result of a misidentification of natural phenomena.
- Due to the flight capabilities of the craft sighted (such as extreme acceleration), and their responses to being chased, it was likely that some, if not all, of the UFOs were being piloted manually or remotely.
- Many of the sightings appeared to be of craft of at least the size of the military's own aircraft.

In 1947, the U.S. Air Force informed its intelligence agents about the phenomenon:

This strange object, or phenomenon, may be considered, in view of certain observations, as long-range aircraft capable of a high

The nuclear test near Bikini Atoll in 1946. This was the first U.S. detonation of a hydrogen bomb. Unlike its atomic bomb predecessors, this bomb resulted in fusing hydrogen atoms rather than splitting them. (Wikimedia Commons)

rate of climb, high cruising speed and highly maneuverable and capable of being flown in very tight formation. For the purpose of analysis and evaluation of these so-called 'flying saucers,' the object sighted is being assumed to be a manned craft of unknown origin. While there remains the possibility of Russian manufacture, based on the perspective thinking and actual accomplishments of the Germans, it is the considered opinion of some elements that the object may in fact represent an interplanetary craft of some kind.

Things did not improve over time. In December 1948, UFOs were spotted near Los Alamos National Laboratory on many occasions. Other sites where nuclear testing and experimentation were going on, like Sandia Base near Albuquerque, New Mexico, also experienced a rash of sightings. All three of the U.S.'s fissile materials production sites (Oak Ridge National Laboratory in Tennessee; Hanford Engineer Works in Washington; Savannah River Plant in South Carolina) also had UFO sightings on multiple occasions. It was as if the pilots of these craft had some kind of fascination for our nuclear testing programs, and, perhaps more disturbingly, knew the location of every such program.

FBI Director J. Edgar Hoover took the matter seriously enough he had a report sent to him. Dated January 31, 1949, it read, in part:

During the past two months various sightings of unexplained phenomena have been reported in the vicinity of the A.E.C. (Atomic Energy Commission) Installation at Los Alamos, New Mexico, where these phenomena now appear to be concentrated. During December 1948...sightings of unexplained phenomena were made near Los Alamos by Special Agents of the (U.S. Air Force's) Office of Special Investigation, Airline pilots, Military pilots, Los Alamos Security Inspectors, and private citizens.

Everyone was seeing UFOs!

Whatever they were, the UFOs continued to buzz these facilities. "Someone" seemed to be intensely interested in the U.S.'s atomic weapons sites, and insisted on conducting unauthorized flights around and over the bases time after time. These overflights were, by witness accounts, done by craft of revolutionary disc-like designs and performed maneuvers in ways no Earth military jet could.

Other Flaps
Many other examples exist. Here are just a few:

- Late December 1944-January 1945, over the Top Secret Hanford atomic materials production plant. From a report dated January 23, 1945, directed to the Commanding General of the Army Air Forces: "The Thirteenth Naval District has made arrangements for Naval Air Station, Pasco, to employ both radar and fighter aircraft in attempting interception of these unidentified aircraft. The airspace over the Hanford Company is both a Danger area and a Restricted area...one incident has occurred since that date [15 January]...attempted night interception again failed."

- In January 1949, green fireballs were observed by scientists, technicians, and military personnel at Los Alamos and Sandia laboratories as well as Camp Hood in Texas.

- Glowing objects the size of ping-pong balls and baseballs were observed at Killeen Base on April 27, 1949. These objects "flew in a zigzag path for a few seconds," and then disappeared. More glowing balls appeared the next day.

- An object that performed zigzag maneuvers as well as right-angle turns and 180-degree reversals in course was spotted at Kirtland Air Force Base in March 1950.

- Disc-shaped objects were spotted over the Nevada Proving Grounds in April 1952. This caught the attention of the media, and it was reported that military personnel and civilians "saw 18 circular objects flying an easterly course which carried them over or very close to the test site...The men watched the saucers for about 30 seconds."

- In 1967, a "round orange glowing object" hovering near the horizon appeared to be interfering in a nuclear missile test with Minuteman missiles (a land-based intercontinental ballistic missile or ICBM). While running through start-up procedures, personnel noted that the object overhead would begin pulsing as soon as the system got close to being operational. One witness said he felt as if the object knew how to disable the system and wanted to make sure everyone at the test knew it as well. After ten to fifteen minutes, the object moved off and tests were able to resume.

Why Haven't We Heard About This?

Robert Hastings, author of *UFOs and Nukes*, notes that, if even one out of every one hundred sightings of UFOs is something truly unexplainable, that leaves a lot of sightings of "aerodynamically-anomalous craft operating in our atmosphere on an ongoing basis." Craft that often seem unusually occupied with militarily sensitive sites. After over seventy years of sightings, "there is no reliable international system for collecting reports, and those that *are* collated…are rarely evaluated, simply because the number of qualified investigators worldwide is so small."

Hastings believes there are, at heart, four reasons this is so:

1. *UFO sightings are unpredictable.* No one can know when a UFO sighting, or even a flap, will occur. Though nowadays people have good cameras in their pockets, it is still true that sightings are often not recorded by observers. Also, the lack of physical evidence, such as a downed craft, means that the evidence for a sighting remains mostly anecdotal, or perhaps backed up by a blurry picture or two.

2. *Scientists have been reluctant to take the subject seriously.* The UFOs have driven the military nuts, but not necessarily the scientists. When it comes to UFOs, scientists rarely took this particular phenomenon seriously, even on the occasion the military was doing so. Dr. James E. McDonald, Senior Physicist at the Institute of Atmospheric Physics at the University of Arizona, said:

From time to time in the history of science, situations have arisen in which a problem of ultimately enormous

> *importance went begging for adequate attention simply because that problem appeared to involve phenomena so far outside the current bounds of scientific knowledge that it was not even regarded as a legitimate subject of serious scientific concern. That is precisely the situation in which the UFO problem now lies. One of the principal results of my own recent intensive study of the UFO enigma is this: I have become convinced that the scientific community, not only in this country but throughout the world, has been casually ignoring as nonsense a matter of extraordinary scientific importance.*

Scientists, or, at least some of them, have indeed labeled those in the UFO community as kooks or publicity-seekers, while in return, the scientists have been labeled presumptuous, intransigent, and incompetent. Clearly, there is no love lost between the two groups.

Scientists may consider themselves merely "skeptical," but others regard them in return as "close-minded." For the skeptics to position themselves as experts on the phenomena that they explain away sticks in the craw of those who believe there is more to know about who is visiting us and why. Including why they want to know so much about our nuclear tests over the past few decades.

3. *The media has not been interested in serious evaluation of the phenomena.* While putting out a piece about strange lights might make an interesting human interest story, for the most part, UFO sightings are dismissed as something to laugh about at the end of a broadcast rather than something that should be taken more seriously.

4. *If UFOs are actually extraterrestrial, the governments of the world might feel they have a vested interest in keeping knowledge of them from the public.* I'm not sure I agree with this one; perhaps some governments might want to keep such knowledge secret, but all of them? For seventy years? This is a bit difficult to buy into, considering how poorly most governments keep secrets. What do the governments buy with all this secrecy? How is it to their advantage? And if it were to their advantage,

how is it that anyone with some blurry footage or a story to tell is able to tell it, often on the internet, to everyone on the planet? This requires us to believe that "the government," by which we mean thousands, if not tens of thousands, of our fellow citizens, know the truth but keep the secret, and are able to stay quiet, but somehow can't take down some YouTube videos. Perhaps it's true that "the government" has knowledge the public at large does not. It does not seem credible, then, that no one has come forward with the proof of extraterrestrial contact after all this time.

In the end, the UFOs are here to stay, and they remain interested in our nuclear capabilities. Hastings says:

> *Perhaps the visitors have empathy for humankind and wish to warn us of the dangers of nuclear warfare. Or perhaps they have a use for our planet, let's say for scientific purposes, and know that global nuclear warfare will disrupt their data-gathering and/or experiments. Even if they only use Earth as a stop-over from their world(s) to their ultimate destination(s)—a manmade nuclear catastrophe might make our world unavailable even to them for hundreds or thousands of years.*

So, is it aliens who are so intensely interested in our development of nuclear weapons and nuclear power? And if so, what is it they really want to communicate by this interest? Perhaps we will find out in the near future, and perhaps it will be the good news that they wish only the best for us, and that their interest in us results in a "positive development for mankind."

Now You See It...But Why?

If we see a sad rain, it doesn't mean the rain is sad, but it means we see it. That's an easily dismissible kind of projection. But what I'm struggling to say, is that we take that rain in through our own hearts and emotions and senses and skin, and all those filters have an impact.
Karen Joy Fowler, Author of *The Jane Austen Book Club*

The senses deceive from time to time, and it is prudent never to trust wholly those who have deceived us even once.
Rene Descartes, Mathematician and Philosopher

I want to be, if I can, as sure of the world—the real world—around me as is possible. Now, you can only attain that to a certain degree, but I want the greatest degree of control. I've never involved myself in narcotics of any kind, I don't smoke, and I don't drink because that can easily just fuzz the edges of my rationality—fuzz the edges of my reasoning powers—and I want to be as aware as I possibly can. That means giving up a lot of fantasies that might be comforting in some ways, but I'm willing to give that up in order to live in an actually real world, or as close as I can get to it.
James Randi, Stage Magician and Professional Skeptic

*
**

The Black Box And You
When movies like *Transcendence* are released (that's the one in which Johnny Depp uploads his consciousness into a computer), someone always interviews people about participating in such a program should it ever exist. Invariably, the person being interviewed will say, "I would

never do that. I don't want to be a mind in a box." The trouble is, that, while they do not appear to realize it, *they already are.*

We don't live in the real world. There. I said it. We just don't. We live in a virtual reality constructed by our brains. That virtual world is a close approximation of the real world, but is not the real world itself.

Think about it. "You" are three pounds of jiggly nerve material held securely inside your skull. Your skull is, for all practical purposes, a box. Your brain sits inside this box, dependent upon your senses to send nerve signals, and dependent upon your nervous system to bring those signals to the brain without altering or fudging them. Your brain will interpret those signals and construct the world around you so that you can pilot your body through that reality. If the information is incomplete, your brain will infer and create information to fill in the blank spots.

To you, this happens in real time. But this is an illusion. It takes time for your senses to send signals to the brain, and for the brain to interpret those signals so that you perceive what you consider to be the "real world" around you. That time lag is short, but it is real.

What *is* this time lag? How long does it take between, say, photons hitting your retina, and your brain telling you there's a dog in the road in front of your car?

These days, researchers can use technology such as functional magnetic resonance imaging (fMRI) and electroencephalography (EEG) to try to discover what the brain is doing. But the approach used by scientists as far back as the mid-1800s has been to simply measure reaction times. Reaction time gives us a real-time idea of how long it takes for a stimulus (say, a starters gun at a footrace) to be sent to the brain, for the brain to interpret the stimulus, and for the brain to get the body to react. For a trained runner waiting for the starter's gun to tell them when they can begin the race, the time lag is about 150 milliseconds.

Interestingly, because the longer the distance between the brain and the source (in this example, the sound of the pistol), and the destination of the action (the runner's leg muscles) means, for very practical reasons, a longer reaction time, it actually does take taller people a few milliseconds longer than shorter people to react to things like the sound of the gun.

But distance is not the only variable. Your nervous system also depends on a few other things:

- Width of the neuron: consider that you can get more cars, and those cars can travel more quickly, down a multi-lane highway than a single-lane road. Similarly, nerve signals will be carried more quickly down wider neurons.

> **Fun Fact**
> Nerve signals traveling down a wide myelinated nerve fiber can travel from 70-120 meters per second, while signals traveling down a narrow unmyelinated fiber might travel only 0.5-2 meters per second. That's like a fire hose versus a trickle!

- Myelination: The coating (myelin) around a nerve cell is also important. Myelin has gaps in it which allow signals to jump from exposed portion of the nerve cell to exposed portions farther along. Because nerve signals are, more or less, skipping the myelinated portions of the nerve cell, those signals travel more quickly down myelinated cells.

- Sheer Number of Neurons: the more neurons a signal passes through, the more time it takes.

Consequently, the signals our senses send to our brain and upon which we depend, take time to arrive and be processed. Fortunately, the time lag is short enough that one can still, say, catch a baseball thrown at over 90 mph. It's only a joke when the ball passes by someone's head and only then do they stretch out their hand to catch it. If we had to experience that much lag on a real-world basis, we'd never be able to function.

But that still means that when we say something like *I saw it with my own eyes*, we are ignoring the reality that we really *didn't*. Our brain received signals from our eyes which it then took some milliseconds to render into an Oculus-type virtual reality for us to experience. This virtual reality is not, and never could be, the objective reality around us, no matter how much we tend to behave as if it were.

So, really, would being a "brain in a box" like Johnny Depp in *Transcendence* be that much different from the reality we experience every day? Our reality isn't reality. We just believe it to be. And most of the time, that belief does not betray us.

Watch Me Pull a Rabbit Out of My Hat

Magicians have known for a long time that the way to get an audience to buy into an illusion is through distraction—get the audience's attention in one place while you do something in another. This was one reason that James Randi, magician and skeptic, suggested that magicians should be a part of any proper investigation into any paranormal claim. Magicians knew how to fool people, while most people are not aware of the techniques used to fool them. When researchers did not take him seriously, Randi took action.

What followed became known as *Project Alpha*. Two young men, both magicians, participated in the newly-formed paranormal research facility at Washington University in St. Louis. They began working with the researchers in 1979.

Randi sent a list of testing requirements to the researchers, asking them to make sure the protocols he suggested were in place in order to help them weed out any hoaxers. He also offered to watch the experiments to see if he could detect any hoaxing himself. His offers were refused. By 1983, Randi judged that the time was right to expose the fraud, and he held a press conference, during which he announced that the two young men were magicians, not psychics. One of them admitted that any so-called psychic tricks he and his colleague performed only appeared to work because "we cheat."

This revelation struck a major blow to parapsychological research. Some decried the deception, while others declared that it had been necessary to reveal to the researchers themselves how easy it was for them to be fooled. The CIA, which was at the time receiving money to fund research into paranormal abilities, was disdainful of Randi's project. Their report, originally written 4 Mar 1983, and released in August 2000 through the Freedom of Information Act, reads, in part:

> *A well-known magician recently released a story to TV and the press claiming that he succeeded in a hoax involving parapsychological research. This magician, Mr. James Randi,*

claimed that parapsychological researchers at an academic facility in St. Louis, Missouri, were taken in by trickery, and that most, if not all of parapsychological research is suspect. These claims are in fact gross distortions...this recent negative publicity should not have any adverse impact on the GRILL FLAME project...It is clear Mr. Randi is solely interested in promoting his image as a clever magician, and in enhancing his career as a showman, at the expense of reporting accuracy. The use of tactics involving "plants" raises significant ethical issues as well...the people used as remote viewers [by the CIA] are not from open public volunteer sources. They have a long-time association with SRI personnel and are known to have extremely high ethical standards.

The ethical standards of Randi, the two magicians, the CIA, and any SRI personnel is hardly the point to be made here—though it is interesting to note that the CIA dismissed any such critique and continued its own research into parapsychological phenomena until at least 1995. Still, the point really is, human brains are only capable of so much. They can be distracted or mistaken for many reasons, none of which necessarily have to do with deception. We depend on our senses. They are simply not reliable.

Invisible Gorillas and Focused Mice

You may have seen the video of a psychological experiment in which participants are shown footage of people passing a basketball in which someone in a gorilla outfit walks through the action.

Those watching almost invariably spot the gorilla, even without being told about it ahead of time. But researchers noted that, when people were asked to engage their minds in a task, such as counting the number of times the people in white shirts passed the ball, fully half of the participants did not spot the gorilla. What is going on here? The gorilla not only walks through the action, but it thumps its chest, stares into the camera, and is on video for nine seconds. Yet, to half the people watching, it was apparently invisible (hence the name for the experiment).

The psychologists in charge of this experiment wanted to show how our brains limit the amount of information they process, and that, at the same time, we do not realize to what extent our brains are doing this. For very practical reasons, our brains do not, and cannot, process everything we see, hear, and otherwise experience via our senses all the time. We would be overwhelmed.

Instead, our brains pick and choose what's important enough to focus on, and what can be discarded. In this case, counting the number of times the players wearing white passed the ball was deemed "important," while everything else was not.

Researchers at MIT wanted to know why and how our brains decide what is important, and how what is designated as important is focused on. They trained mice to understand that flashing lights and certain sounds were directions on how and when to run. They also trained the mice to understand a different signal, which was to tell them to disregard the previous signals. By the end of their experiment, they realized that the mice brains were not becoming more excited by the commands, but actually became more inhibited. It was as if the brains of the mice were focusing by *dialing back*

A mouse. Because they're too stinking cute not to be included here. (Wikimedia Commons)

on everything that was not judged to be important to the task at hand (or paw). Instead of ramping up the excitation levels in areas of the brain that needed to have more focus, the mouse brains turned down the excitation levels everywhere else. It was as if you were trying to listen to one radio station among four, and instead of turning up the volume of the one you wanted to listen to, you left that volume alone and turned down the volume on the other three instead.

The trouble is, of course, that sometimes our brains get it wrong. We focus on something that isn't important, while missing something that is.

Eyes on the Prize

Eyewitness testimony is essential to many criminal cases, and to nearly every, if not every, UFO sighting. While corroborating physical evidence, such as scorched grass or photographs, can help, people expect to hear the story of "how it happened" from the person who was there. We want to know what someone experienced before we evaluate whether or not something is true.

However, once again, human minds are all too easy to distract or deceive—even when we're not trying to.

It might seem that humans have, overall, pretty good memories. We are able to memorize poems, remember complicated sets of directions, and navigate our way through the world without constantly being reminded of where we're going or how to get there.

People often have a sense that their memory is like some kind of video, recording everything around them, and that if they just *try hard enough*, they'll be able to remember tiny details or even larger chunks, of a memory that seems spotty. This attitude can be reinforced by fictional works, where characters like Sherlock Holmes can tell ordinary humans that they "see but do not observe," while he, presumably, is capable of observing the world around him in ways no one else quite can. Fictional characters also reassure each other with sentiments like "you have the memory, you just can't access it right now." This is great when the author can write the characters however he or she wants, without regard to how biology and psychology work in the real world.

However, people do not function like fictional characters. Researchers have discovered that, unlike something stored in a single place or in a single continuous "file" (so to speak), memories are reconstructed, like a jigsaw puzzle, from various pieces stored in various places in the brain. Every time you remember something, it has to be recreated from bits and pieces. Your sense that it is a "whole" memory is merely a bit of self-deception on the part of the brain.

There are even those who claim that your memory of an event is not the actual memory of the event, but the memory of the last time you reconstructed the event, which makes your memory even more removed from the actual time and place of the original occurrence than you probably thought possible! That does not make me confident about anything I think I recall well, and am relatively confident did actually happen. Did I really have a bandage on my toe on my first day of school? I think I did. Is there any way to verify it? Well...my mother probably took a picture (it was my first day of school, after all), but that photo might not show my feet. Could I establish the presence of a bandage any other way? At this point, no.

Ultimately, the question is, can we rely on our memories at all? Bits and pieces of jigsaw-puzzle like images and sounds and smells cobbled together to the best of our neurons' capabilities. Is that a memory? Is it even real?

The short answer there is: no, it may not be. Researchers in the Netherlands asked people about a 1992 crash of an El Al cargo plane into an apartment building. Despite the fact the event was not captured on film, many study participants who were asked "did you see the television film of the moment the plane hit the building?" said that they had. In fact, 55% of them said that they had, though the number had changed to 67% when the participants were asked later in a follow-up survey.

Undeniably, a plane did hit an apartment building. No doubt the people did remember getting the news. However, they could not have remembered seeing a video of the event because such a video does not exist. Yet they claimed to remember seeing it.

These people aren't lying. They do believe they recall something they could not possibly recall. They are constructing a memory that was suggested to them by the researchers asking a leading question (note that participants were asked *did you see the television film* and not *did you hear the news on the radio* or even *how did you get the news?*). Witnesses were able to fill in details of the crash as if they had witnessed the event, because their brains could logically determine what must have happened, at least to some extent. Our brains like to "fill in the blanks," and will do so, especially with a tiny bit of encouragement.

McGurk and Yellow Strawberries

But there's more going on inside the brain. It isn't just "filling in the blanks" when it doesn't have all the information it thinks it should have. The brain also makes choices when it has sensory data that conflict. Do your eyes see one thing, and your ears hear something different? Or can you "see" the way your meal is supposed to taste? It turns out, your brain makes choices that can be difficult, if not actually impossible, for you to override.

If you haven't been exposed to the McGurk Effect, you can easily expose yourself to it by searching for a video on the effect on YouTube. In short, though, the effect shows the viewer someone saying "fa fa fa" but the audio is saying "ba ba ba." No matter how much you may want to hear "ba ba ba" you will only hear "fa fa fa" when that is the motion the lips are making.

This illusion appears to affect anyone, even if they're told what's happening. The brain, getting one message from the ears but another from the eyes apparently chooses the visual information as correct by default. Close your eyes and you'll hear "ba." Open them, and the "ba" immediately morphs into "fa." According to Lawrence Rosenblum of the University of California-Riverside, a researcher who has been studying this for twenty-five years, he has never been able to hear "ba" when watching "fa." *Not once in twenty-five years.*

Similarly, the brain will also opt for believing visual information over taste. Serve a chef a glass of water colored yellow and flavored with lemon, and the chef will be able to tell you what he or she is tasting. However, hand the same person a glass of yellow-colored water but flavored strawberry and he or she may be completely baffled. Even though, one would think, a chef ought to be rather good at distinguishing tastes no matter the situation. I know that's what *I* would expect.

However, taste is strangely mercurial, depending on visual input. Researchers have discovered that, if one asks participants which drink is sweeter, a red drink or a green drink, they will choose the red drink, even if the green drink actually has up to 10% more sugar in it. From that, I infer that having more than 10% additional sugar in the green drink overrides the visual information. So if you'd like to drink something sweet but don't want so many calories, why not formulate a low sugar drink for yourself—just make sure it's red!

In another case, a mouthwash company found that users rated their orange mouthwash as less astringent than the blue, even though the formulations were exactly the same.

So what?
Sadly, this means that we humans are subject to making a lot of mistakes. Honest mistakes, sure, but mistakes nonetheless. Color affects our taste.

Visual information can override what our ears are hearing. Memories have to be reconstructed every time they are brought to mind, and can be not only reconstructed, but constructed *ex nihilo* when our minds don't hold the information, but can infer it.

But that's not even the end of the sadness iceberg when it comes to the psychological and sociological effects that swirl around incidents like Roswell.

Roswellian Syndrome

Remember how the Roswell incident largely disappeared for thirty years and then re-emerged as a mysterious event, having shed its original "weather balloon" explanation? The process by which this happened has happened elsewhere, but because Roswell is the most famous example, some call this "Roswellian Syndrome." This is a five-step process by which ordinary events become entangled in extraordinary narratives.

Step 1: Incident.

Clearly, the first thing that happens is that...something happens. In the case of Roswell, something described as a "weather balloon" came down in a field. The Air Force has since admitted it was a balloon which supported "box-kite-like radar reflectors" made of sticks and foil. It was these bits of sticks and foil, some covered in tape, which were later described by witnesses, and which the military found and collected. The balloon and the radar reflectors it had carried aloft were part of Project Mogul.

Project Mogul was an attempt by the U.S. Air Force to see if there were a layer of atmosphere that could detect the sounds of explosions thousands of miles from the source. A layer of the ocean had been discovered by researchers from Columbia University and Woods Hole Oceanographic Institution which could do this, so it seemed likely the atmosphere had a similar layer. To discover whether or not this was true, researchers launched weather balloons dangling these "box-kite" bits of foil-covered sticks. In the end, other means of listening, such as using seismic sensors and air sampling, proved more accurate than weather balloons. Project Mogul was shelved.

Step 2: Debunking

Although the sheriff originally had a more fanciful explanation for what was found in the field, and the local paper enthusiastically declared the military had collected parts of a "Flying Saucer," most people were clear that what crashed had been a balloon, and that the things collected were ordinary items like foil. At this juncture, no one seems to have been deliberately lying or hiding evidence or participating in any organized deception.

Step 3: Submergence

As mentioned, the Roswell story pretty much disappeared for thirty years. The lack of a story of the unusual or bizarre or proof of any lying on the part of the military were probably part of the reason why no one showed much interest in Roswell until the 1970s. However, as interest in UFOs and government cover-ups began to take off during that decade, people who remembered the original incident decided it was high time to take another look, and figure out what really happened at Roswell in 1947.

Step 4: Mythologizing

Here's where the heavy lifting really starts. Once an incident, even one as relatively normal and conspiracy-free as Roswell was for thirty years, gets some major attention, the story may take on a life of its own. This may be because people are simply mistaken, or because they are perpetrating a hoax, exaggerating the original events and/or reports, and possibly confabulating with local folklore. With Roswell, several of these factors came into play.

Memory, as has been mentioned, is fallible. The longer it has been since an incident, the more likely some details will have changed or even been rearranged, not because a person deliberately wants to misremember, but just due to the way our brains work, including how they fail to work as we age. An anthropologist from Texas Tech, Curry Holden, began speaking about having led students to the Roswell crash site and having retrieved both the flying saucer and its dead occupants! However, his family said he had never told *them* that. They also pointed out that he was ninety-six when he made this revelation, and his memory had become unreliable.

Another person, this one who claimed to have been part of the military unit that had retrieved the downed craft, was a known hoaxer.

The man, Major Jesse Marcel, was known to have lied about his own background: for instance, he claimed to have a college degree; he claimed he'd received medals for being a pilot in World War II who had shot down many enemy aircraft; and he also said he had been shot down himself—all known lies. He also claimed the sticks found at the crash site "were not wood" and that they had hieroglyphics on them, by which he was apparently referring to the floral design on the Scotch tape.

Marcel and Holden weren't the only ones adding to the narrative. Now stories were brought forward about the alien occupants of the craft, who, depending on the source, had been removed to Wright-Patterson Air Force Base in Dayton, Ohio, or Area 51 in Nevada, or to some other facility. Even into the 1980s, continued attempts to attach new revelations to the Roswell story, including the infamous "alien autopsy" film, made headlines and drew ratings on television.

Step 5: Reemergence and Media Bandwagon Effect

By now, nearly all the pieces were in place to produce an epic modern folktale, both widely known and disseminated. Books began to be written about Roswell, including *The Roswell Incident*. Documents, including the "MJ-12" papers, surfaced. Newspapers and reviewers looked at such things uncritically, for the most part. The dust jacket for *The Roswell Incident* includes language describing how the authors "uncover astonishing information that indicates alien visitation may actually have happened—only to be hushed up in the interest of 'national security.'" Instead of merely being described as giving a factual account of what he saw, the original witness was now portrayed as someone who had been forced to lie; in fact, he had "gone to great pains to tell the newspaper people exactly what the Air Force had instructed him to say."

Moving On From Roswell

Roswellian Syndrome didn't just affect the Roswell incident. Other incidents, which were not necessarily seen as mysterious at the time, have been resculpted into major "evidence" for UFO encounters.

An incident in Pennsylvania which was previously referenced as having been one where the crash remains had odd hieroglyphics which some claim now match those showing up on military drones, is another case in point. According to some researchers, the UFO made changes in course as it was crashing before finally going down near Kecksburg, Pennsylvania.

At that time the incident happened in 1965, no one seemed to have an issue with the object being described as a meteor. But in 1990, the story was dug up and rebranded on NBC's *Unsolved Mysteries*. Now, instead of a meteor, the object had become something metallic, acorn-shaped, and had been retrieved by the military and taken to Wright-Patterson (where, I suppose, it could join the equally fictitious Roswell crash components and dead crew). The story that bodies had been recovered from the Kecksburg crash site was later retracted by the person who made the claim.

Joe Nickell and James McGaha also note the infamous Rendlesham Forest incident, which was originally described as a streak of light passing overhead that appeared to crash into the forest. Other people also reported a light that night, and it was well-known that a meteor had passed by.

An added wrinkle was that the eyewitnesses who saw the UFO that night described it as "pulsing" and that it was doing so every five seconds. When others investigated, it was discovered that, from the vantage point of the eyewitnesses, the Orfordness lighthouse was visible, and that it flashed at five second intervals. The witnesses had certainly seen something real—it just hadn't been a UFO.

> ### Not-Quite-A-Fun Fact
> The Orfordness lighthouse was demolished in July 2020. So, if you're someone who likes to visit sites of odd reports, be aware you won't be able to see the lighthouse yourself, unless you have a time machine.

As with Roswell, books and articles began to come out on the incident, though unlike Roswell, which took around thirty years to be mythologized, Rendlesham took three years. It started with a story in the British tabloid *News of the World*, and was titled "UFO Lands in Suffolk—and That's Official." The legend grew from there. Now there were rumors that a particular military official had met three humanoid aliens during the Rendlesham incident—though the man himself denied this had happened.

The Results of "Roswelling" a Sighting

The somewhat sad (or, at the very least, disappointing) thing about finding an older case that was, at the time, not terribly mysterious, and then trying to make it so, is that this takes away attention from anything that might really be going on.

Assuming that incidents like Roswell, Kecksburg, and Rendlesham were no more than originally reported—i.e. military balloons and meteors—then any attention and time given "investigating" them is time wasted. Are there actual UFOs in our skies? Could aliens be visiting us? We'll never know if researchers are distracted by incidents which shouldn't even be on the radar.

Why would people do this? Perhaps they genuinely think there was a governmental cover-up. Perhaps they are looking for a way to get a television show off the ground. There may be all kinds of reasons that sightings become mythologized. The trouble is, while this may be advantageous for a particular author or researcher, it does nothing to move any serious research forward.

On the positive side, developing new folklore can lead to the formation of online communities, the development of fun little museums that play off the legends, and gatherings like the Mothman Festival in Point Pleasant, West Virginia and the annual MUFON conference.

In a world where people are often worried about their jobs, their finances, and (in a post-COVID age), their safety during a pandemic, watching UFO researchers on television interview witnesses and chat about sightings can be an entertaining distraction, as can the books, articles, and websites one can read and ponder.

That may not be the positive everyone is looking for. But when the world we live in is also full of humans with easily-fooled senses and faulty memories, we have to accept that sightings will happen, and that most, if not all of them, will be nothing more than a misidentification.

The question is, what if some of them aren't? First, we need to know what people are misidentifying.

It's a Bird! It's a...Skyfish?

Everyone wants to be informed honestly, impartially, and truthfully, and in full accordance with their views.
Gilbert Chesterton, Author and Philosopher

I think we risk becoming the best informed society that has ever died of ignorance.
Ruben Blades, Panamanian Musician, Composer, and Politician

The only real mistake is the one from which we learn nothing.
Henry Ford, Industrialist

**

Do You Want to Believe or Do You Want to Know?

Anyone who's seen more than a couple episodes of *The X-Files* remembers the poster on Fox Mulder's office wall: it was a picture of a UFO and the caption read *I Want To Believe.*

The thing is, Mulder already believed.

He's in good company. Gallup conducted a poll of over fifteen hundred adults in the United States asking about their views on UFOs. They found that the statement "some UFOs have been alien spacecraft visiting earth from other planets or galaxies" was agreed upon by 33% of respondents, with a higher percentage in the West agreeing with that statement than in the Midwest.

That may not be a majority, but it indicates that it is likely that *one hundred million* Americans believe UFOs exist and are alien.

But before we can find the sightings that might be alien, we need to be aware that there are other things in the sky which can be mistaken for a UFO.

Clouds

This one may seem too easy, but clouds are one of the main things people mistake for alien spacecraft.

Lenticular clouds over Boulder, Colorado. (Wikimedia Commons)

One kind of cloud in particular, *lenticular (lens-shaped) clouds,* are often the culprits here. These clouds form when winds blow across mountains. Winds at differing heights, but blowing in the same direction, can give the clouds interesting saucer-shaped layers. Other clouds, known as *hole-punch* clouds, form when super cooled water droplets held aloft are disturbed. The super cooled water instantly freezes, and then falls from the sky. Hole-punch clouds are dramatic, though unlike lenticular clouds, it is the *hole* in the cloud being mistaken for a UFO, not a cloud itself. You can find some fantastic images of both lenticular and hole-punch clouds with a Google search.

The International Space Station and Other Orbiting Bodies

Humans are remarkably bad at telling how near or far something is to them when the object is in the sky. Even airline crews have been known to report an object approaching their aircraft when radar confirms the object is over one hundred miles away. Consequently, it is unsurprising that the International Space Station, as well as other satellites, have often been mistaken for UFOs flying by overhead. One of the most common cases of mistaken identity is that people spot Naval Ocean Surveillance System satellites (which are in groups of threes) and describe them as black, triangle-shaped UFOs.

One of the more interesting ways a satellite can be mistaken for something else comes from the sixty-six Iridium communications satellites currently orbiting our planet. These satellites have highly reflective antenna. When those antennae reflect sunlight down to the surface of the earth, an observer in the right place will see a brilliant flash. This flash may last for several seconds, and will outshine everything else in the sky.

> **Fun Fact**
> You can find out when the ISS will be over your position by going to spotthestation.nasa.gov and putting in your location. By doing this, I found out that the next time the ISS passes overhead is in five hours!

Planets

Perhaps the number one case of mistaken identity is Venus. People are unprepared, and, I suppose, surprised to see something so bright, and decide it must be something extraordinary and not just another planet. In a way, this is not unusual, as Venus is the brightest object in the sky except for the moon, and it can only be seen at certain times of the year and only at late evening or early morning. So people, especially those who don't watch the sky regularly, may go months or years in between sightings.

But people have been known to mistake Jupiter and Saturn for UFOs as well, especially when they appear close together. The fact that objects in the sky appear to "follow" you as you travel (a phenomenon people are most familiar with when it comes to the moon) can explain many reports where a UFO "tracks" the observer.

One of the ways researchers discover that the observer has mistaken Jupiter, Saturn, or Venus for a UFO is that the UFO will only appear to them when the weather is clear. One witness, upon joining a UFO researcher when it was overcast, told him, "We almost never see them on nights like this."

If a witness can provide concrete times, dates, and direction they were looking when they saw a UFO, it can be possible to discover if Venus or another planet were in that area of the sky that night. Unfortunately, witnesses often aren't clear on when things happened. They might admit it was "a few weeks ago" and that they were looking in a southerly direction sometime after sunset. This will not be enough information to find out if they saw a planet, a satellite, a meteor, a bolt of lightning, an airplane, or something equally non-mysterious.

Strangely, the one object one would think everyone would recognize is the moon, and even it is not immune to being mistaken for a UFO. One case occurred in southern Wales in 2007, where a woman called the police to report that something had been hovering over her house for half an hour. A patrol was sent to investigate and radioed back later to report that the moon had been the offending object.

Military Aircraft, Drones, Flares, and Other Things
Though of course the military does not divulge what sort of tests it is doing at its various sites, it is entirely possible that people are sometimes spotting experimental aircraft, missile, or other equipment being tested by the military. While the Phoenix Lights sighting in 1997 are still believed by some to be legitimate UFO sightings, the lights have been attributed to military flares used during training exercises.

Camera Issues
Just like many ghost photos turn out to be wrist straps or thumbs, many UFO photos turn out to be created by something very ordinary, usually due to operator error.

If you turn your camera toward something extremely bright, like the sun, the light will overwhelm the sensor and the bright object will appear black. I have seen videos online where excited observers tell how they can't see the UFO with their eyes, yet it is being recorded as a black disk by their cameras.

Diamond-shaped UFOs are also often a result of not understanding the camera. These shapes result from the

> **Fun Fact**
> Interlacing occurs because people want better frame rates without needing to use more bandwidth. The video records every other line on the image, and then goes back and records the other lines. (So, say, at first it records lines 1-3-5-7, then 2-4-6-8.) Thus, something moving very quickly will not be in the same position by the time the video is recording the alternate lines. This can result in a weirdly stretched-out object inside the image. Though some organizations would like to see interlacing discontinued, it is still used. Progressive scan, unlike interlacing, records each line in sequence (1-2-3-4-5-6-7-8).

internal aperture attempting to get a handle on a distant object when the light is uneven. The camera has difficulty focusing on something when it can't adjust to the lighting conditions, and so the aperture opens and closes in a futile attempt to bring the image into focus.

But my favorite in-camera type of UFO is the skyfish ("rods"). When these white streaks show up in a video, they are generally a surprise, as the person taking the video had not witnessed them at the time the video was taken. That is because skyfish result from interlacing, and are generally the result of things like dragonflies zipping by the person taking the video.

I was genuinely sorry to find the explanation for the skyfish, because I really wanted to encounter one myself.

I am upset I will never see a skyfish.

Oh, Those Angels!

Radar angels have been around since radar was invented. These "angels" are blips in the radar signals that often triggered alerts, especially in the early days.

One of the first, if not *the* first incident involving radar was in March 1941 in Britain. Britain had the most advanced radar system at the time, but that didn't mean it always worked perfectly. On that night, five different radar facilities noted that a significant number of blips was headed for the coast from Europe. These blips remained on the screen for at least two hours before simply fading away. They returned the next night, and this time, technicians were called in to check the equipment. Two nights of masses of blips headed for Britain that remained on radar screens for hours and then disappeared? And then no enemy aircraft were ever actually spotted? That was troubling.

Technicians were unable to solve the issue. Massive formations of blips continued to plague radar stations for weeks. Eventually, officers began to fear the Germans had some kind of secret device that might be able to send false signals to the British stations, and that once the British became used to them, the Germans would launch an all-out invasion, only, by that time, no one would be concerned with another night of blips on the screen until the actual bombers were overhead and it was too late.

This, obviously, never happened.

No one was ever able to figure out exactly what was going on, at least not during the war itself. One officer later recalled that "we were busy fighting a war [so] we spent no time investigating." He also made a joke about how the blips must be a supernatural phenomenon, since they were visible one minute, and disappeared the next. He said they were the "souls of British soldiers killed in France over the centuries returning to defend their country."

The idea was fanciful enough that, by 1947, even the Oxford English Dictionary adopted the term and listed *unexplainable echoes on radar screens* as "angels."

These radar angels continued to plague the system, even after it was upgraded in the 1950s. Sometimes, so many angels appeared on the screen, the radar systems were useless. Ground observers were unable to distinguish actual RAF planes from the dozens, if not hundreds, of blips that were...something else.

In February 1957, an investigation was launched to finally determine what the blips were. After two years, the study concluded that the angels were due to flocks of birds. This explained why blips were more common during the birds' autumn and spring migrations. It also explained why blips were often more common at dawn, when birds left their overnight roosts and flew outward from a central point in search of their morning meal.

Radar equipment was recalibrated to ignore objects as small as birds, and after the 1950s, such radar angels became far less common. By the 1960s, angels became a thing of the past.

However, investigators had learned that radar *could* be fooled. Simply because a piece of scientific equipment "saw" something did not mean that the object was unidentifiable, only that it was unidentified. The idea that a radar blip *must* be something metallic and solid was popular for a while, but has now also became something relegated to the past. Technology is great, and has improved our lives immensely, but it is still as fallible as the humans that created it.

The Sky is Falling!

Chicken Little was right, at least some of the time. The sky *does* fall, sort of.

Some of the more famous meteor showers take place during the same period every year, because the Earth is passing through the remains of things like the tails of comets. Whatever debris the Earth encounters burns up in the atmosphere. Meteors, and UFOs, often occur during the Perseid shower (late July-August); the Leonid shower (November), and the Quandrantid shower (early January). Usually, such showers are best observed during a new moon, or any time the moon is not full, and will appear to originate in a certain section of the sky. It is difficult to see anything from large urban areas these days due to light pollution. Get far enough away from a large city, wait until after midnight on a moonless (or near-moonless) night, and you, too may spot a spectacular light show overhead.

A bright meteor over Germany in 2019. Photo by Dorian Cieloch. (Wikimedia Commons)

Meteors can appear as streaks of light, or as larger streaks that crumble and fall apart, or as flashes as bright as the full moon, sometimes described as "fireballs." These especially bright meteors (bolides) often seem to trigger UFO sightings, as calls to the police about some kind of mysterious craft passing by overhead often coincide with the occurrence of a bolide meteor.

Now what?

Part of the trouble of identifying objects in the sky is that we're no longer used to watching the skies. While people used to be more intimately aware of the world around them, including the layout of the constellations and appearance of things like meteors in the skies, we spend more time now indoors watching television or doing other chores in our artificially-lit abodes. Darkness is not something we are used to.

But even if we go outside, we may not see much overhead. Perhaps 99% of the people living in North America and Europe can no longer see the Milky Way when they look at the night sky. Our home galaxy, the source of many legends and myths, has faded from our view.

This means many people never experience true darkness. It may also be interfering with the lives of various animals: some animals navigate by the stars, including the Milky Way; dung beetles actually orient themselves by spotting the Milky Way; what happens to the natural world when the Milky Way itself is gone from the sky, not because of anything the universe did, but because of the human propensity to light everything up.

As time goes on, humans get more and more cut off from the world around them. Electricity and central air/heat have reduced our need to be outside. We look down at phones instead of up at the sky. We eat pre-packaged food and have no idea how to grow our own anymore.

While we could see these things as tragic, to a large extent, they simply *are*. But it does mean that when something appears in the skies over our heads, or something we can't identify is outside the house at night, it is all too easy to think *aliens* rather than knowing it's just the raccoon that got into your garbage last week, or a flash of light off a satellite that is making sure you have a cell signal 24/7 in your new, tech-driven, life.

Are We Alone? Or Just Lonely?

The interesting thing is why we're so desperate for this anesthetic against loneliness.
David Foster Wallace, Author of *The Broom of the System*

Loneliness is, and always has been, the central and inevitable experience of every man.
Thomas Wolfe, Author of *Look Homeward, Angel*

I said it's a cold universe and I don't mean that metaphorically. If you go out into space, it's cold. It's really cold and we don't know what's up there. We happen to be in this little pocket where there's a sun. What have we got except love and each other to guard against all that isolation and loneliness?
David Chase, Producer of *The Sopranos*

✳
✳✳

Here We Are

There's a scene toward the beginning of the movie *Battleship* where scientists rejoice in sending a signal out into the universe to see if we can, eventually, get a signal back. It's like sending a message in a bottle. But instead of an ocean, we're sending that signal into the inky blackness of the void of space.

There's one scientist, of course, who sees a problem with this. What if the aliens we contact aren't friendly? Then what do we do? "It'll be like Columbus and the Indians. Only we're the Indians," he says quietly.

It's a movie, so of course we get an answer (much more quickly than would make sense, but this is a movie designed around explosions, not plot). And, yes, the aliens are decidedly not friendly. We never figure out exactly what they want (is that even important?), but we do know they're hostile.

In an episode of *The Big Bang Theory*, Sheldon ponders the likelihood of hostile aliens coming across a message from Earth and interpreting it to mean we're fleshy and tasty.

Many people may remember the plot of the *Twilight Zone* episode "To Serve Man," in which we discover the aliens wish to eat us. The fact that the aliens actually came here to harm us was so unexpected that it is able to serve as the plot twist.

In the 1970s, however, humans seemed to be overwhelmingly hopeful about contact with aliens. Maybe men walking on the moon had gotten a bit old by 1972, but space itself had not. The Viking landers were designed to look for life on Mars, though the experiments they conducted found nothing definitive. The Voyagers carried messages that would ultimately leave the solar system and tell our story to whomever might find them. Movies like *Close Encounters of the Third Kind*, which featured aliens that seemed only curious about us, raked in millions of dollars. Aliens, their ships, and their signals, were everywhere—movies, television, books, scientific papers, NASA budgets, Congressional hearings. UFOs were squarely in the zeitgeist.

But the 1970s were hardly the first time people had wondered if, or even simply assumed that, aliens existed out there in space.

Huygens to the Space Age

Four hundred years ago, Christiaan Huygens posited that the universe held "so many Earths, and every one of them stock'd with so many Herbs, Trees and Animals...even the little Gentlemen..." William Herschel felt he saw forests on the moon. He even theorized that sunspots were holes in the sun's atmosphere, and that underneath them dwelt civilizations of advanced beings.

Percival Lowell is still well-known for seeing canals on Mars, which are now believed to have been nothing more than the blood vessels of his own retinas.

In 1938, Orson Welles famously panicked many people in the country by dramatizing an invasion from space. Although many think the broadcast didn't frighten as many people as has been claimed, it did make my grandmother run to the neighbor's house in concern that something awful was happening in New Jersey.

In all these cases, the fact that there was alien life in the universe was simply assumed. No one seemed to think this was such a stretch. I suppose, if there were life here on Earth, then why not everywhere else? It just seemed to follow.

But then we began to send out probes. And radio signals. We began SETI, the Search for Extraterrestrial Intelligence.

The occasional anomalous signal (like the infamous "Wow! signal") got hopes up, but ultimately, proved to be fleeting and non-repeatable. If the Wow! signal was the work of aliens, they have been quiet ever since.

And now, decades on, we have exactly zero evidence that we are anything but alone. The Wow! signal was recorded in 1977, after all. That's pushing forty-five years ago.

> **Fun Fact**
> You can see what the SETI Institute is up to by checking out their website at www.seti.org. They haven't found alien life yet, but they want to know "Where will you be when we find life beyond Earth?"

More recently, there have been several glimmers of hope, one being the periodic dimming of Tabby's star, which is in the constellation of Cygnus. This dimming was odd in that the periods of dimness did not follow any pattern and did not seem to be happening due to planets crossing in between the star and observers on Earth.

It didn't take long for someone to theorize that a Dyson sphere could be the reason for the star's random dimming. That excited enough people that "Dyson sphere" undoubtedly became a much more widely-known (and widely-Googled) term than it ever had been before. In short, a Dyson sphere is a megastructure built around a star to capture as much of its energy as possible. Though Freeman Dyson popularized the idea in the early 1960s, the idea was originally proposed in a 1937 novel by Olaf Stapledon.

Sadly, most scientists feel the possibility of a Dyson sphere around Tabby's star is extremely unlikely, and that what we're seeing are dust clouds. But who knows? The dust cloud theory has its detractors, too. (Take that, dust!)

Waving to the Martians

Mars has always been one of the main, if not *the* main, location where we have looked to find alien life. It has an atmosphere, it's large enough to have a decent amount of gravity, and we now know it used to be covered in water (which may now be locked up beneath the surface). When Percival Lowell thought he saw canals bringing liquid water from the poles to the cities on the equator, people did their best to imagine what it must be like to live there. Edgar Rice Burroughs delighted plenty of people with his books about the American Civil War Veteran John Carter's adventures there with several trippy alien species and the love of his life, Dejah Thoris.

People were prepared to learn more about life on Mars. But the more we observed, the less likely life seemed to be. The atmosphere might be too thin. Mars lacks a magnetic field so solar radiation bathes the surface. Liquid water no longer exists on the surface, and hasn't for an estimated three billion years. This might mean that, despite the liquid water, the early life of the planet was still simply a barren one.

> **Fun Fact**
> What is the Perseverance rover's main mission? According to NASA, it is to "seek signs of ancient life and collect rock and soil samples for possible return to Earth." Check out facts about Perseverance at mars.nasa.gov/mars2020/mission/facts/

However, for those with a bit more hope, it seems that the first one-and-a-half billion years of Martian evolution might have meant that microbial life could have had time to develop. This life either died when liquid water disappeared from the surface, or it went underground with the water. Our newest rover on Mars, Perseverance, is designed to help satisfy our curiosity on the subject of life elsewhere.

The blasted surface of the planet, as it stands now, is no place for life. Dejah Thoris is not waiting for her Earth-born husband in the wild sands of Barsoom. Which is kind of a shame.

Howdy...Neighbor?

Mars, at least for now, appears to be a bust. And today, few (if any) astronomers think we will find alien life on another one of the planets of our solar system, though, as well see later in this chapter, we haven't given up hope. Now our attention has mostly turned toward the moons in our system as the places where life might be found.

Europa, one of the moons of Jupiter, is one of the main places scientists theorize we might find life. After all, it looks like Europa might have the main ingredients for supporting life. It is likely to have liquid water in oceans under its icy surface. Warmth could be supplied by the tidal flexing by Jupiter's gravity, keeping the ocean from being frozen solid. It's also possible that the moon's water contains enough oxygen to fuel chemical reactions with other elements and molecules in the ocean, or that exist in the zone between the liquid water and the frozen crust. For now, all we know is that this seems possible. Whether or not Europa actually harbors life is unknown, and if it does, it is likely to be single-celled organisms like bacteria.

Titan, a moon of Saturn, is another place that might harbor life, though this is a bit less likely than life on Europa. As far as we know, there is no liquid water on Titan, at least on the surface, but it does have a thick atmosphere. The presence of an underground liquid water ocean has been theorized. On the surface, though, anything liquid is methane and ethane. This liquid makes the surface of the moon *look* Earth-like, in that the flowing methane and ethane have carved river channels and filled large lakes.

The mystery of Titan is why there is methane in its atmosphere. Sunlight will break down methane rather quickly; therefore, little methane should be present. Yet there it is. On Earth, higher-than-expected levels of methane mean organic life. As sunlight destroys some, it is replaced by this life. On Titan...who knows? All we know is that we do not see what we expect. Exactly why we don't is one of the solar system's puzzles we've yet to solve.

One of the most exciting new developments lately was the discovery of phosphine in the atmosphere of Venus (I did mention getting back to planets that may harbor life, right?).

Why was this important? Quite simply, on Earth, phosphine is created by microbes. If this gas is also in Venus' atmosphere, that might be an indicator of microbial life, then. Very exciting stuff!

However, some have questioned the data. Is the gas detected even phosphine? Some say it's simply sulfur dioxide. Others have looked at the data and said that the amount of phosphine is not nearly what was originally claimed, and that the tiny amount in the atmosphere might be created by natural processes.

How can we find out for sure? It could take a while.

Japan has a satellite currently orbiting Venus, but it does not have the capacity to test for phosphine. The Indian Space Research Organization is planning to send a probe to Venus; the probe is currently scheduled to launch in 2025. In the meantime, we are stuck with using telescopes on our planet to try to decipher the enigmas of an atmosphere millions of miles away.

Until there is more proof, the mystery of the phosphine in Venus' atmosphere remains just that. Tantalizing evidence that there *might* be life somewhere else on our planet, but even if there is life, it will be microbial in nature. That will still be a great discovery, should it ever happen, but it does not get us closer to having neighbors we can chat with, or even visit with as we stop off for refueling while exploring the outer reaches of our solar system.

Our dream of being one of two (or several) intelligent races in our solar system remains only a dream.

If the UFOs are indeed from another world, it does not seem that such a world can be found orbiting our sun.

We Want Aliens!

It follows that, were we not so keen to find aliens, we would have stopped looking some time ago. NASA could have pointed to its Viking missions and said, "nope, no life on Mars," and moved on to something else. They could have shrugged and said, "Water on Europa? Maybe, but you think there's life there? Probably not." UFO sightings would have lessened over time, one would think. After all, we had some curiosity on the subject, nothing in particular came to light, and now we're moving on.

But that isn't what happened. We are still looking. We are still seeing things in the sky. We are still watching aliens on television and in the movies, and dreaming about meeting with them someday.

NASA, worried about the possibility of bringing alien microbes to Earth, as well as taking Earth microbes other places, has had stringent guidelines in place to attempt to keep such things from happening. After all, we wouldn't want to be wiped out by bacteria from Mars, would we? And if we contaminated Europa, how would we know later if the microbes we found there were native, or were the descendants of the ones we ourselves brought along?

The concern was such that the probe Juno was directed to plunge into Jupiter's atmosphere on the theory that this would be the best way to keep any Earth microbes that might have stowed away from contaminating the Jovian system. For practical, as well as personal, reasons, we have been anxious to find alien life, and to know, when we've found it, that it is truly alien. The day Perseverance, or another rover, or another probe, discovers incontrovertible proof of alien life, it would seem most of us will be excited, and will rejoice, even if the life ends up being the smallest bit of virus or bacteria-like life. We will finally know we're not alone.

Briefly, in 2017, the world was electrified by the news that something had entered our solar system. Dubbed 'Oumuamua, it almost seemed like the ship from Arthur C. Clarke's *Rendezvous with Rama*, in which an alien ship drops into our solar system, briefly wakes up and recharges, and then heads back out into the void.

'Oumuamua was unusual for several reasons: it appeared to have come from interstellar space; it was ten times more reflective than a typical "space rock;" it had a cigar-like shape rather than being spherical; and, most interestingly of all, it *sped up* once it had passed our sun. The increased speed was more than could be accounted for by the sun's weakening grip on the object. Within a few weeks, 'Oumuamua had continued on its journey, with us none the wiser as to its true nature or origin.

While most scientists have been chary about saying more than 'Oumuamua could certainly be a natural object, the fact that is was far stranger than any object we had yet encountered means there have been some who have posited that it was a relic of some alien technology. Perhaps a race of long-dead aliens launched it into space billions of years ago, and we were simply one of the solar systems it has visited on its lonely journey.

It is likely we will never know.

Maybe We're Just Lonely.

For humans, being alone is a terrible thing. There is a reason one of the worst punishments we can inflict on another person is to ostracize them, to make them suffer *aloneness* for a time—maybe years, maybe forever.

Timothy Taylor took a look at certain caves where early humans placed some of their dead, and noticed that the individuals buried in those caves did not represent a cross-section of society. They were the very old, the very young, the infirm, and the crippled. Missing were the young and healthy who might have died in childbirth, or due to a hunting accident, or simply from a disease. In other words, he saw that some people were selected for a cave burial, and the selected ones were those who, in some societies, would have been on the margins. The cast-offs. The ostracized. He theorized their

Some of the author's ancestors and other relatives at a family reunion ca. 1930, Hamburg, Illinois. Photo from the author's personal collection.

cave burials had not been to ensure their continued presence (as ancestors) with the group, but to *exclude* them from this. These people didn't get to go where all the young, healthy people got to go when they were unfortunate enough to die young due to injury or illness. These ostracized ones were forbidden the afterlife everyone else was believed to have, and deserve. Knowing how keen people are to belong, it would seem, includes knowing the cruelty of cutting them off, even after death, so that they never belong anywhere.

Which is just an example of how important it is for us to be part of a web of interpersonal relationships. There's a reason peer pressure works, after all.

A few years ago, researchers wanted to know if there were any reason for the institution of marriage that was true for every society. If one society said that marriage was for raising children together, and another society didn't do that, they marked that reason off the list as not being universal. In the end, only one reason remained on the list. As far the researchers could determine, the only reason given by every society that has the institution of marriage to justify that institution is that it brings you in-laws. In other words, it increases the number of social bonds you are a part of, and can take advantage of (say, for food or safety). Increasing the number of groups in which we take part is, therefore, absolutely one essential that every human society agrees is important.

Is it so odd, then, that, instead of being frightened, some humans might rejoice at the idea of meeting another species with whom we could discuss philosophy, love, culture, and science?

The Third Man

The fact remains that humans are social creatures. We can't get around this factor of our biology. We must have companionship to maintain our sanity, perhaps even to remain alive. To help us, it would seem we have an adaptation inside our own minds which helps us in times of dire emotional and physical stress. This is what many call the Third Man, and which John Gieger refers to as "the angel switch."

The phenomenon of the Third Man is absolutely fascinating to me. The term refers to a mechanism by which our brain literally "throws" its voice to provide an external source of advice when we are alone. Do our brains come programmed with the ability to *invent* companions out of thin air when we desperately need them?

How often have people reported that they have been contacted mentally by UFOs and/or their occupants? Perhaps these people have been contacted telepathically by aliens, but they may also have had an experience with this Third Man. Perhaps, for some reason, the "angel switch" deep in their minds was triggered.

The term came to into use after Ernest Shackleton's disastrous Antarctic expedition where he and two companions climbed over mountains to get to a whaling station where they hoped to be able to acquire help for the crew they'd left behind. Later, when they compared notes, they admitted that each felt like a fourth person was with them, even though they could not see this person. T.S. Eliot used this idea in his poem *The Waste Land*, though he cut the number of people down to two men and one invisible companion, and wrote of it, *Who is the third who walks always beside you?*

Generally, the Third Man contacts people who are either in, or who are about to be in, dire straits. You're a mountain climber who might die due to a change in weather? A voice over your shoulder may tell you to get off the mountain. You're a scuba diver who has lost the guide rope after a swirl of silt blocked your vision? Maybe a voice speaks to you and tells you to swim to the left. Sometimes, the Third Man is a voice over the left shoulder, sometimes the right. It can sound male or female, but also it might sound like neither.

This voice clearly could easily be identified with a guardian angel, for those who believe in them, but aliens using telepathy might be what "guardian angels" have been all along. However, the most obvious explanation is that the brain itself is warning you of your peril. Perhaps the mountain climber noted some subtle shift in the weather but ignored the signs. Perhaps the scuba diver would have remembered to look to the left for the guide rope had they managed to calm themselves down.

In the introduction to *The Third Man Factor*, Vincent Lam reveals his own experience with the Third Man. He was exhausted and stressed from studying for exams which would make or break his entrance into medical school, and then had a visitation.

I sensed a presence. It did not alarm or frighten me because, like many in this book, I knew immediately that the presence, or Third

Man, wished to help me. I felt that my guardian angel had been sent by God to guide me at a difficult time. The angel spoke to me and gave me advice. I decided to record some of this valuable advice. I...sat down at the computer, and wrote several pages of guidance that was directly dictated by the angel's voice. Strangely, when I went to look for those pages of advice, to review what I had been told, I could not find them.

It may be that humans are able to conjure companions at will, or it may be that we have the capacity to receive messages from otherworldly visitors, who wish only to guide us on our way.

Is the time right?
Humans don't just need others, we may need others *more* in the past few years than ever before.

A 2018 survey by the insurance company Cigna found that nearly half of all adults in the U.S. report feeling alone "sometimes" or "always." Forty percent reported feeling "isolated." This concerns many psychologists because feelings of loneliness and isolation increase the risks of people using adverse coping mechanisms, like smoking, overeating, or drinking, to try to cope.

"There is robust evidence that social isolation and loneliness significantly increase risk for premature mortality," said Julianne Holt-Lunstad, PhD, a professor of psychology and neuroscience. While we don't know whether or not loneliness is worse now than ever before, we do know that more people live alone than did in the past.

Couple the percentage of those who feel lonely and isolated with the current drop in volunteerism and involvement in community organizations such as churches or clubs, and we may have the perfect storm: more people living alone precisely at the point in history where social institutions are fraying. Holt-Lunstad said, "Being connected to others socially is widely considered a fundamental human need." This need seems increasingly not to be met.

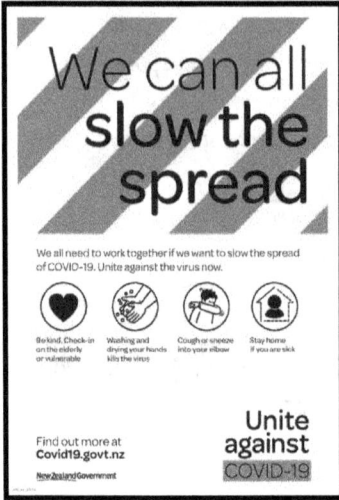

A poster from the New Zealand government informing people on how to slow the spread of COVID-19. Staying home and obeying social distancing protocols have helped contain the virus in areas where these actions were encouraged, but have also resulted in people feeling cut off and lonely. (Wikimedia Commons)

The COVID-19 pandemic certainly has not helped. Now, social distancing is the norm, and being able to socialize with others has been strongly discouraged when not actually forbidden. People are wondering, will I ever eat in restaurants again with the same carelessness I did before the pandemic? Will I be willing to shake hands with others even when we're all vaccinated? Can I stand to work in a job where I have to deal with the public?

As people become more isolated, are we simply looking to the skies for the companionship we are missing from our culture, which appears to be divesting itself from the institutions that used to bind people together?

Maybe the aliens are filling a hole in our hearts that used to be filled by other humans. That's a downer of a thought.

Big Ships and Small Bots

Nanotechnology will let us build computers that are incredibly powerful. We'll have more power in the volume of a sugar cube than exists in the entire world today.
Ralph Merkle, Computer Scientist

The sightings always recede to the edge of what technology allows you to do. The aliens are kind of keeping pace with technology.
Seth Shostak, Senior Astronomer for the SETI Institute

As technologies of flight evolve, so do the descriptions of unidentified flying objects. The pattern has held in the 21st century as sightings of drone-like objects are reported, drawing concern from military and intelligence officials about possible security threats.
Greg Eghigian, Professor of History, Pennsylvania State University

$$*\!*\!*$$

UFOs Over Time

UFOs are not new, but their form may very well be. Over the centuries, people have described the odd things in the sky in different ways, as the UFOs have evolved to appear more like what we expect to see now than what people expected to see decades, or centuries, ago.

Though originally seen as "wheels" or other intriguing objects, UFOs got a bit more real-world when, in the late 1800s, they began appearing as airships. Some described them as being steam-powered. Others noticed they had propellers. A few came equipped with searchlights. It's not difficult to see why people were choosing such things as technological marvels. The 1800s had been a time of great change: telegraphs, photography, steamboats, trains, even weather balloons, had entered people's lives. One could send a message across the country in seconds. Or ride a machine from coast to coast. If we were going to see people from other worlds and their technology, it only made sense that they were at least as technologically advanced as we were.

But as airships became more common in real life, UFOs needed to up their game, apparently. As weapons like the V-1 and V-2 rockets and nuclear bombs came into being, UFOs began to take on more rocketship-style appearances. They flew, but not quite like Earth aircraft. Kenneth Arnold described his encounter with the "flying saucers" as "I could not find any tails on them. I felt sure that, being jets, they had tails, but figured they must be camouflaged in some way so that my eyesight could not perceive them."

By the 1950s, we have the saucer-shaped UFOs that were so easy for people to hoax with street light covers or hubcaps. These objects did not appear to need tails or wings, or other features the aircraft we were more familiar with needed to fly. Their propulsion systems were a mystery. How they could travel as quickly as they did without some visible means of propulsion, and without aerodynamic requirements like wings and tails, caused both fascination and dismay. After all, if we could not understand their means of getting around so quickly (remember that Kenneth Arnold had calculated the ones he saw were traveling at over 1700mph!), and if we could not follow them due to the impossible maneuvers they could apparently achieve without visible effort, how could we defend against them? What if they had weapons? What if they attacked or invaded?

Even more disturbing was the question of, why were they flying over now? What did they want in the late 20th century they did not apparently want before?

Many people thought that our development of nuclear weapons was the trigger. When we became a species that could harness the atom, we suddenly became much more interesting, or even a possible threat, to those beyond our own planet. We were inventing technological marvels that aided us, but at the same time, we were busy ratcheting up our ability to conduct war far more terribly than ever before.

UFOs go Triangular, and More!

UFOs continued to evolve. They became black triangles, huge and silent, that glided over cities. David Marlor, author of *Triangular UFOs: An Estimate of the Situation*, says he has investigated *more than 17,000 cases of black triangles!* That's a helluva lot of sightings of just that one sort of UFO! These sightings are not limited to the United States. Black triangles have been reported over the United Kingdom and Czechoslovakia, among other places.

Black triangles have been reported in different sizes as well. Several were seen (or one was seen on multiple occasions) over the Hudson Valley between 1983-1986, and were described as being 100 yards from tip to tip. However, the triangle that hovered over Puerto Rico in 1969 was a mere one-sixth that size at fifty feet in diameter. One of the ships spotted during the Phoenix Lights episode in 1997 was described as being "three football fields" in size, which would put it at 300 yards, three times the size of the Hudson Valley craft(s).

Despite being so large, even the 100-yard ships have distinctively non-Earth-like capabilities. They may hover, or alternately, make crazy maneuvers, like right angles, that can't be accomplished by an Earth craft without banking. They can accelerate so quickly that they don't go from zero to sixty in five seconds, more like zero to 1000 mph instantaneously. One Belgian air force colonel was quoted as saying that the data their computers gave them on the craft they were monitoring "exceeded the limits of conventional aviation."

The National UFO Reporting Center claimed that, from January-June of 2020, over 200 black triangles had been reported. So black triangles appear to be here to stay.

But black triangles aren't the only shape out there now. In footage recently released by the Pentagon, small white oblong shapes now known as Tic Tacs were observed by the FLIR (Forward-Looking InfraRed) system on some of the Navy's F/Ao18 Super Hornet aircraft flying over the United States' eastern coast. The Tic Tac most usually cited when describing the reports was allegedly forty feet long, had no noticeable source of propulsion, being a simple white oblong shape, and exhibited similar extraordinary maneuverability to the black triangles. The pilot who claims to have coined the term Tic Tac in relation to the object said:

The thing that stood out to me the most was how erratic it was behaving. And what I mean by "erratic" is that its changes in altitude, air speed, and aspect were just unlike things that I've ever encountered before flying against other air targets. It was just behaving in ways that aren't physically normal. That's what caught my eye. Because, aircraft, whether they're manned or unmanned, still have to obey the laws of physics. They have to have some source of lift, some source of propulsion. The Tic Tac was not doing that. It was going from like 50,000 feet to, you know, a hundred feet in like seconds, which is not possible.

However, there are those who have a more down-to-Earth explanation for the Tic Tac. Seth Shostak, an astronomer at SETI, noted that the Tic Tac style UFO was observed after an upgrade to the jets' FLIR systems. Bugs are something we're all familiar with, especially when something is new or recently upgraded. That doesn't mean the Tic Tac was, in fact, a glitch, only that *glitch* is a likely explanation. The incident, however, apparently made the Navy think about working on new guidelines to help pilots report encounters with objects they could not identify.

However, the Pentagon would like to let it be known that these craft, while *unidentified*, are not necessarily extraterrestrial. As quoted by New York Times, "No one in the Defense Department is saying that the objects were extraterrestrial, and experts emphasize that earthly explanations can generally be found for such incidents."

Tic Tacs may be the radar angels of the twenty-first century, but they are still a curiosity, and so far, no one really knows for sure what they are.

The Costs of Space

Here's why many people simply can't accept there are aliens zipping around in physics-defying spacecraft: cost.

As far as we can tell, the speed of light is an absolute speed limit in our universe. The sheer difficulty of making a craft that could even get near the speed of light is something so overwhelming, we simply can't see how it could be done. But, even if we could make a ship that could accelerate to, say, 0.99999 the speed of light, the distances in space are so great it would still take years, even thousands of years, or tens of thousands of years, to get anywhere.

Supposing you could do that, you would think you'd have some significant mission parameters that would need to be fulfilled before it was time to begin the millennia-long journey back home. What would you be doing, then? Testing the environment to see if it's suitable? Surely you could have figured that out largely back home. After all, we can learn at least some things about exoplanets right here from the comfort of our home planet.

Would you waste time just buzzing around doing nothing? Why? What information could you be gathering that requires doing so from rural locations where perhaps only one person might see, or be contacted? Why not simply land somewhere publicly, tell what you have to tell, a la *The Day The Earth Stood Still*, and then go home? Or stay to help?

Shostak says, ""If the aliens are here, you gotta say they're the best houseguests ever, because they never do anything. They just buzz around. They don't address climate change; they don't steal our molybdenum."

Various theories have been put forward that the aliens are here to welcome us to a galactic federation of species, or to help us overcome our primitive natures, or some such, but if so, they do not seem to be going about this in a way that makes any sense. Again, why not land somewhere obvious and just *tell us what they want*. If they're so powerful that they have ships that can cross interstellar distances, then surely they could keep us from destroying ourselves in an initial panic at ships landing in front of the U.N.

Somehow getting a 300-meter-wide black triangle from one star system to another would surely cost too much in terms of fuel. I don't know what kind of mass such a ship would have, but accelerating it to a significant portion of the speed of light, then decelerating it, would be a huge undertaking.

Perhaps it is with that in mind that movie aliens are often here to steal our water so they can use it as fuel (*Battleground: Los Angeles, Oblivion, Independence Day*, among others). But that begs the question, why bother with Earth? There's billions of times more water in the Oort Cloud than exists here, and it's free for the taking. You can just scoop it up at your leisure in whatever quantity you want or need.

Some movies try to get around this by saying the aliens want liquid water. Well, then why not suck Europa dry? No pesky humans to bother you way out there. Why come all the way to Earth for the piddly amount we have here and have to deal with creatures that do, after all, have nuclear weapons? And, in any case, it's not like "space is cold" is news to any spacefaring race. Surely, if they needed water, they would have to assume whatever they were going to find was going to be solid, and build their ships accordingly with huge defrosters, or engines that could run on the frozen stuff.

No matter how you slice it, interstellar travel is, as far as our understanding at the moment, not practical. At least not for ships the size of the ones being reported.

But if aliens had gone in the other direction, they might have better luck exploring the galaxy.

Nano Means Small, Really Small
Nanotechnology is relatively new. The idea behind it was proposed in 1959, but it wasn't until much later, as our technology improved, that it was anything more than an idea.

In short, learning to use nanotechnology means learning to deal with matter on a very tiny scale: the scale of the atom. If scientists could control atoms to develop machines the size of

> **Fun Fact**
> How small is a nanometer? Well, you might think a sheet of newsprint is pretty thin, but it is 100,000 nanometers thick!

molecules, all kinds of amazing things might be designed. Such as:

- Very strong, yet very light cables, might be able to be created which would give us the ability to get things into space with a sort of "space elevator." This elevator would ride up and down the nanotech-created cable.
- Cures for cancer could be designed that were geared to seek out and destroy only cancer cells. For instance, cancer cells often have larger pores in their cell membranes than regular

somatic cells. If the nanotech cure was too big to fit into a somatic cell's pore, but just the right size to slip into a cancer cell's pore, ordinary cells would remain unaffected while cancer cells would be destroyed.

- Machines could be created with moving parts only a few atoms in size, enabling them to be utilized in places where machines normally could not be sent. Perhaps they could repair larger machines, or even people!

- Sensors only a few atoms in size might be able to detect foreign substances in a city's water supply, or in someone's blood, and send back signals to let the people observing know what it had detected.

And, when it comes to space, we could space probes the size of houseflies, or even smaller. These could be designed to a tolerance of one-billionth of a meter. They might be self-replicating and self-repairing. We could send them out into space and wait for them to bring back information on the solar systems around us. Something only a few atoms big could reach near light-speed with much less effort than something the size of several football fields. The nanobots could also know how to use the hydrogen atoms they find around them as fuel. In the end, we might not leave this planet, but our ultra-tiny machines might.

It would make sense, then, that alien civilizations would have reached similar conclusions, and would have realized that it was far cheaper, and more practical, to send nanobots to explore their galactic surroundings, not full-sized ships staffed with crews that need to eat, respire, and do all the things normal organic beings do. Even if the crew of the ship(s) could be stored cryogenically for the journey, their life support systems are still going to have to be maintained. The ship might freeze the atmosphere and let everything stay in deep cold, but at some point, the crew will need a livable environment. The ship will have to warm up, regenerate the atmosphere, get water, food, and waste disposal functions running, and then wake the crew from their frozen slumber without damaging or killing them in the process.

It would be easier simply to send the machines. Especially if they were only a few atoms big.

Suits and Stiff Faces

Any reasonable person with access to all the information about UFOs would become a firm believer.
Henry McKay, American Sociologist

If the masses started to accept UFOs, it would profoundly affect their attitudes towards life, politics, everything. It would threaten the status quo. Whenever people come to realize that there are larger considerations than their own petty little lives, they are ripe to make radical changes on a personal level, which would eventually lead to a political revolution in society as a whole.
John Lennon, Singer and Songwriter

The one thing the darkness of secrecy cannot tolerate is a spotlight shining on it. And the more of us holding the light, the better.
Steven M. Greer, UFOlogist

⁂

<u>The Last Suit You'll Ever Wear</u>
Surely most of us have seen the 1997 film *Men in Black* or one of its sequels. In it, members of the eponymous organization must save the world from alien invasion again and again while remaining entirely anonymous and while wearing their signature black suits. The look appears to be modeled after agents in federal organizations like the FBI, who tracked down the "FBI's

> **Fun Fact**
> The FBI started their Most Wanted list in 1950, and it's still active today. Go to fbi.gov/wanted/topten to see who's on the list now.

Most Wanted" while wearing similar attire.

It didn't take long after the first post-World War II UFO sightings for similarly clad men to begin confronting witnesses with vague warnings about staying quiet about their experiences. The detail of the mysterious "Men in Black" was part of the Maury Island sighting in 1947, and, although that sighting was later discovered to be a hoax, it is interesting that the hoaxers decided to add the detail of the Men in Black to their story. They must have known it to be a detail that UFO stories sometimes included. Or they simply felt their story would carry more weight if the government had sent agents to get involved.

During the 1940s and 1950s, sightings of the Men in Black began ramping up. Awareness of the phenomenon took a leap forward when UFO researcher Albert K. Bender told his story. Bender, the founder of the International Flying Saucer Bureau (IFSB) shut his organization down rather suddenly in 1953 shortly after announcing that he had news of a significant breakthrough in UFO research and would reveal it in an upcoming newsletter.

An FBI agent makes a phone call on a portable device ca. 1939. I'd include a picture of the real Men in Black, but they are famous for their camera-shy natures. (Wikimedia Commons)

Recounting the incident years later, Bender said that he had reneged on his announcement that he would reveal something startling and revelatory, because he had been visited by "three strange men in black suits." He said the men who approached him spoke to him telepathically and weren't from our world. Bender also claimed that invisible aliens were present when he was interviewed about his Men in Black experience by other UFO researchers, and that he could not reveal what these invisible entities wanted or where they were from.

I guess that makes sense. Men in Black are notoriously *not* invisible, but who wants to reveal something when an invisible alien might be standing at one's side, marking what one says, and judging if one has gone too far in revealing the terrible truth that must not be spoken?

In any case, once he had made the decision to shut down the IFSB, Bender offered refunds on those who had paid for a subscription to his newsletter, saying:

A source, which the IFSB considers very reliable, has informed us that the investigation of the flying saucer mystery and the solution is approaching its final stages...The mystery of the flying saucers is no longer a mystery. The source is already known, but information about this is being withheld by orders from a higher source...We advise those engaged in saucer work to please be very cautious.

We might note that 1953 was sixty-eight years ago, and that the "solution" to the "flying saucer mystery" is still pending. Perhaps the aliens, or the government, or the Men in Black, have been distracted by some other duties or issues.

Beyond Bender
Eventually, Gray Barker wrote the book *They Knew Too Much About Flying Saucers*, which he published in 1956, and in which he recounted stories from UFO researchers on how they'd been approached, even threatened, by Men in Black. He wrote, "Three men in black suits with threatening expressions on their faces. Three men who walk in on you and make certain demands...after they got through with you, you wished you'd never heard of the word 'saucer.'" Weirdly, these individuals often know about the observer's experience before he or she can even report it, and sometimes, before the experience even happens! The Men in Black are also singularly well-informed about the witness(es), being able to reveal more about them than any stranger would know. Clearly, the Men in Black had vast resources at their disposal for surveillance and intelligence-gathering.

Of course, in the 1960s, it was more difficult to have a lot of information on a single ordinary person. These days, the Men in Black would merely have to check Facebook and Instagram to learn all kinds of things that, in decades past, strangers would simply not know about a person. In fact, if the Men in Black exist, I am sure they are behind most of the quizzes on Facebook that ask you for your favorite animal, ice cream flavor you'd never eat, and how many broken bones you've had in your life.

Before the internet, though, the stories about the Men in Black followed similar lines: a UFO researcher comes across something *real*, something that might prove that UFOs are an actual thing, and not just swamp gas or mass hysteria or misidentified military aircraft. But no sooner has the researcher found this terrifically important piece of evidence than they are approached by three Men in Black. After this visit, the UFO researcher recants his claims and the evidence is never released. Sometimes, the researcher doesn't reveal until years later why he suddenly backtracked on his announcement that he had the goods on UFOs, and sometimes he never reveals it at all, leaving it to others to surmise that his silence is due to a visit from the Men in Black.

Nearly twenty years after releasing his book, Barker was continuing to develop the Men in Black narrative. In 1975, he issued a warning to those on his mailing list, "If you are accumulating too much information in a certain UFO subject...better not read these contents!" Which, of course, only made people want to read the contents even more. Barker clearly knew how to sell some books and magazines, which he was doing through his Saucerian Press.

Barker died in 1984, but an organization called "New Saucerian Press" is keeping his books in print.

Identifying Men in Black

Perhaps the most significant thing about the Men in Black is that they are, well, *men in black*. But beyond that, there are other attributes people have reported about them.

Men in Black generally seem to arrive at their destination in threes, though stories of them operating as pairs, or even as one person acting alone, have been reported. Early on, Men in Black had a tendency to identify themselves as members of the U.S. military (generally the Air Force), which caused the Air Force to send out a memo in 1967 telling everyone to "immediately notify the Office of Special Investigations if persons masquerading as military officers were apprehended intimidating UFO witnesses."

Not every encounter with the Men in Black has been reported as threatening, but the majority have been. The Men in Black have even been known to stop a witness' children on their way to or from school to warn them that their parent should stop researching UFOs. A university professor using the pseudonym "Max Radar" claimed that, once his children had been approached, he left the university to go into hiding.

Police officers who have chased UFOs have been told never to reveal what they saw (apparently the threat didn't work or we wouldn't have their statements). For those, especially in the early days, who managed to snap a photo, such evidence of the UFO either mysteriously disappeared or was confiscated by the Men in Black.

The Men in Black have even threatened people's lives. Dr. Herbert Hopkins, who had conducted hypnosis sessions with UFO witnesses, was approached by the Men in Black who warned him that Barney Hill (of the infamous abduction case) died "because he knew too much," and that Dr. Hopkins would meet a similar end if he continued with his research. He was instructed to destroy all the recorded hypnosis sessions and any other research he had done on UFOs or else. He apparently did as instructed.

These men (it's always men) appear either too neat, as if their suits had never been previously worn, or they may appear dirty and wrinkled. Some have been described as walking with an odd rocking gait, as if their hips were not constructed in the same way as human hip joints. Others claim they stagger as if drunk. Their voices are oddly stilted and very distinct. One person described the man he saw as "sitting down very mechanically."

John Keel, UFO and cryptid researcher and author of many books, described his encounters with the Men in Black like this:

> My telephone ran amok first, with mysterious strangers calling day and night to deliver bizarre messages "from the space people." I kept rendezvous with black Cadillacs on Long Island, and when I tried to pursue them they would disappear impossibly on dead-

end roads. Throughout 1967, I was called out in the middle of the night to go on silly wild-goose chases and try to effect "rescues" of troubled contactees. Luminous aerial objects seemed to know where I was going and where I had been. I would check into a motel at random only to find that someone had made a reservation in my name and had even left a string of nonsense messages for me.

Clearly, the Men in Black had a thing for leading John Keel on, either because it amused them, or to distract him from his research. They do not seem to have threatened him, at least overtly.

Where Do They Operate?
By far, most of the Men in Black experiences occur in the United States. Margaret Sachs claims that they "rarely" appear in other countries. However, Raymond E. Fowler recorded a Men in Black incident which apparently took place in Mexico City. John Keel claimed they had been spotted "from Sweden to Spain, Australia to South Africa." So, it would seem, they are not strictly limited to showing up within the territorial boundaries of the United States; yet, they do seem to show a marked interest in the U.S. over other areas of the world.

A Different Take
On at least one occasion, a Man in Black appears to have been encouraging UFO research rather than trying to cover it up. This report was recorded in 1982 with the witness recalling an incident from just two years prior.

According to the witness, he was doing research on UFOs in a university library when he was joined by a somewhat dark-skinned thin man with sunken eyes. The man wore a dirty suit that needed to be ironed and which was too big for the man's thin frame. The man also wore a bolo tie, which is an intriguing detail.

The man engaged the witness in conversation about what he was researching, and then asked if the witness had ever seen a UFO. The witnesses explained that he had not, and that, while he enjoyed the stories, he wasn't particularly interested in whether or not UFOs were actual physical objects like alien craft. The man in black became quite agitated and began speaking loudly (remember, this is in a library), saying "Flying saucers are the most important fact of the century, and you're not interested?"

The witness was alarmed and tried to calm the man down. Eventually, the man did calm down, got up awkwardly from the table, put his hand on the witness' shoulder, and told him, as a sort of benediction, "Go well in your purpose," before departing. The entire incident upset the witness to the point where he kept his head down and did not watch the odd man depart.

Black Helicopters

How do the Men in Black get around? Usually, it's in old-style cars (often Cadillacs) painted black, which habit goes along with their old fashioned 1930s-era suits and fedoras. But sometimes, the Men in Black use more modern equipment, such as helicopters.

Black helicopters began to be featured in UFO stories at some point in the 1970s. They became so much a part of the culture that Idaho Representative Helen Chenoweth said that, even though she'd never seen one, enough of her constituents had that, "I can't just ignore it."

It's not as if helicopters that are black don't exist. In fact, they are regularly seen flying around Area 51 in Nevada. A reporter from the Ottawa Citizen was sent to camp outside Area 51 for a couple of nights and discovered that the assignment "did not disappoint." While he was there, "a number of black helicopters zipped over Nevada Hwy 375, and headed toward the base. The choppers, which flew only 30 meters above the ground, had no identifying markings."

However, the use of black helicopters by secret organizations such as the Men in Black has never been substantiated, whatever Representative Chenoweth's constituents think. Still...it's a better way to get around than in an old-timey car, right?

Unless you're a classic car buff, in which case, perhaps not.

The Real Men in Black?

Perhaps the most credible theory about the Men in Black is that they did (or do) exist, at least sometimes, and that they are from various branches of the U.S. military. In this case, the Men in Black turn out to be agents spreading disinformation.

In the 1970s, a man named Paul Bennewitz had his life ruined by these actual Men in Black. While living near Kirtland Air Force Base, Bennewitz began picking up unusual signals on his radio equipment, and kept spotting odd lights in the sky. Far from assuming the radio signals and the lights were from Kirtland just across the road, Bennewitz began theorizing that these odd phenomena were actually extraterrestrial in origin. He reported his findings to the Air Force.

The Air Force realized Bennewitz hadn't picked up on E.T. but he *had* picked up on *them*. Instead of trying to shut him down, however, they encouraged his fantasies and fed him false information. Within a few years, Bennewitz had discovered various alien languages, had found alien technology (actually props dropped in his path by Air Force personnel), and had discovered a downed UFO in the hills while flying a small plane. He began to obsess about an alien invasion that was surely coming.

Bennewitz was so wrapped up in his fantasies that he was eventually committed to a psychiatric facility by his family. Perhaps the Air Force personnel who had been stringing him along got a good laugh out of that, but for the rest of us, we can only hope driving one man insane was a good return on keeping whatever was actually going on at Kirkland a secret. Otherwise, we have to assume the real Men in Black are military personnel who get their jollies out of cruelty.

So, They Exist...Or Not?

Well, clearly, Men in Black have been reported for years, so in some sense, yes, they do exist. But is there an actual agency? Or is this phenomenon simply something the military engages in when they want to point civilians in a different direction? Misdirection is, after all, a classic tactic, not just for con artists and stage magicians, but for the military as well.

Some more interesting explanations for them are that they may be a kind of tulpa (thought-forms). Terrorists, or the FBI, or some other group or agency, causes us so much anxiety, that we have created "tulpoidal forms stabilized by collective fear." That our collective insecurities and anxieties might be manifesting in the real world is certainly an intriguing theory, and could explain many things about UFOs and Men in Black quite easily (assuming tulpas exist and can be so created). That's one I hadn't heard before.

More than likely, Men in Black, when they do exist, are trying to get people to look in the wrong direction, as they did for Paul Bennewitz. Far from trying to keep contact with aliens a secret, they are covering for purely terrestrial military secrets by encouraging the invention of stories about aliens and recovered technology.

Out From the Shadows

We are part of a symbiotic relationship with something which disguises itself as an extra-terrestrial invasion so as not to alarm us.
Terrence McKenna, Ethnobotanist and Mystic

On the day that we do discover that we are not alone, our society may begin to evolve and transform in some incredible and wondrous new ways.
Carl Sagan, Astronomer

There is something irreversible about acquiring knowledge; and the...search for it differs in a most profound way from the reality.
J. Robert Oppenheimer, Physicist

Any fool can know. The point is to understand.
Albert Einstein, Physicist

Knowledge is an unending adventure at the edge of uncertainty.
Jacob Bronowski, Mathematician and Historian

✲
✲✲

Where are the Insiders with the Knowledge?
One of the most frustrating things about being a UFO researcher, one would suppose, would be the ongoing lack of good data. Pictures are fuzzy, radar contacts could be glitches in the system, eyewitnesses can't give concrete details as to date, time, and place of a sighting. And if someone *does* manage to get some good data, here come the Men in Black to confiscate it.

Seriously, what's a researcher to do? Why don't those who are in the know come out and admit what they've seen, or reveal what evidence they've hidden from the public all this time?

It seems some of them are coming out of the woodwork these days. Although they don't seem to have changed the game much yet, perhaps they will.

> **Quote**
> *There is no evidence, I wish to emphasize, that these life forms from elsewhere are hostile toward us, but there is a great deal of evidence that they are concerned with our hostility.*
> Steven M. Greer

In 1950, a retired Marine Corp Major, Donald Keyhoe, published an article called "Flying Saucers are Real." In it, he was critical of the way the military was conducting UFO research, and claimed that our planet had been "under systematic close-range examination by living, intelligent observers from another planet." He later expanded that article into a book of the same title.

Because Keyhoe was retired military, his book attracted some attention. *Life* magazine published an article called "Have We Visitors From Outer Space?" The original head of Project Blue Book, Captain Edward Ruppelt, also wrote a book, *The Report on Unidentified Flying Objects*, which he published in 1956. Ruppelt said:

> *Every time I begin to get skeptical I think of the other reports, the many reports made by experienced pilots and radar operators, scientists, and other people who know what they're looking at. These reports were thoroughly investigated and they are still unknowns. Of these reports, the radar visual sightings are the most convincing. When a ground radar picks up a UFO target and a ground observer sees a light where the radar target is located, then a jet interceptor is scrambled to intercept the UFO and the pilot also sees the light and gets a radar lock on only to have the UFO almost impudently outdistance him, there is no simple answer.*

Full Disclosure Project

In 2001, Dr. Steven M. Greer held a meeting at the National Press Club to try to get the ball rolling on government disclosure as to what is known about UFOs and their occupants. The meeting included various men who had been involved in various military and other security agencies, such as Richard Doty, William Uhouse, Stephen Lovekin, John Callahan, and others, who claimed to have been part of the government cover-up since at least the 1960s. Greer is an ex-emergency department physician who left that career to go full time in pursuing his goal of getting the government to release whatever information they have on UFOs and alien contact.

At this 2001 meeting, the panelists disclosed some of the bases where crashed craft and their occupants (usually dead and mangled from the crash, but sometimes not quite dead) were relocated. The bases indicated as the main storage areas for these items were the ones everyone had previously suspected hosted alien artifacts: Kirtland, Wright-Patterson, and Los Alamos. They also revealed that the government had captured and kept a single living alien, which was about four feet tall, had four fingers on each hand and suction cups at the finger tips, and which allegedly lived in captivity several years before dying in 1952.

This alien had been one of several recovered in the late 1940s at a crash site (though it had been the only one recovered alive). Apparently, there are many such UFO crash sites. An unidentified speaker in the documentary said, "One of the briefing officers that was taking us around, talking about what was going on, they said there had been over one hundred crashes in the Four Corners area."

Pretty intriguing stuff! Though it does beg the question of how alien pilots, flying advanced craft that can outperform our aircraft at every turn, end up crashing so often. Especially in the same area! Is there something about the Four Corners area that confuses alien pilots and/or their ships' navigation systems?

Major George A. Filer, III, a retired Air Force intelligence officer, described an incident over Wiltshire, England where planes were sent after a UFO. He said that, upon meeting Prince Philip some time later, he discovered the prince had been fully informed of the situation. "He knew all about the fact that we had chased the UFO. He kind of made me a believer in a sense...when someone of his stature indicates that they're real and probably from another planet, it's very convincing."

The 2001 meeting did not seem to have the effect Greer wished. Though many people gave testimony, until I watched the documentary *Unacknowledged*, I had no idea the meeting had even happened, or that retired military personnel had been so willing to share their stories way back in 2001.

Greer hasn't given up. He wrote a book and released the documentary, both under the title *Unacknowledged*, in 2017. In April 2020, a documentary covering similar material, *Close Encounters of the Fifth Kind: Contact has Begun*, was released.

More Whistleblowers Come Forward
Another whistleblower has stepped out of the secrecy shadows recently. Luis Elizondo, former military intelligence officer, came forward in 2017 to tell his story. Unlike Greer, a physician, Elizondo, as a military officer, had more insider credibility. His work performance review in 2016 declared that he was an exemplary officer and that his "importance...to national security...cannot be overstated."

At nearly the same time, Chris Mellon, who had served as deputy assistant secretary of defense for intelligence under Presidents Bill Clinton and George W. Bush, came forward to discuss what he knew. In an op-ed in the *Washington Post* in early 2018, he claimed that "The military keeps encountering UFOs. Why doesn't the Pentagon care?"

Between them, Elizondo and Mellon got UFOs taken more seriously, at least by some in the media; "And so, in the span of a few months, a topic long confined to the

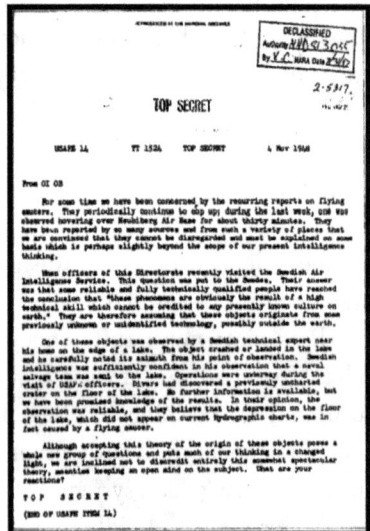

A document labeled Top Secret from November 1948 concerning a crater caused by a UFO at the bottom of a lake in Sweden. The document was declassified in 1997. (Wikimedia Commons)

tabloids and fringe media had become a serious news story." Still, both men were a bit wary of publically declaring that UFOs were alien. Elizondo said, "My personal belief is that there is very compelling evidence we may not be alone," though he stopped short of claiming that "not alone" meant *extraterrestrials* exist. Mellon said, "I did not claim the objects were alien. Merely real, intelligently controlled, and not ours— hence the need to investigate further."

Much like Keyhoe before them, Mellon and Elizondo have had difficulty getting the Pentagon to admit to anything. They have been frustrated by institutional secrecy and disinterest. "We cannot afford to avert our eyes, given the risk of strategic surprise," said Mellon in his 2018 op-ed.

Elizondo is unhappy with the rumors that have followed him for the past several years. "I did not do this for frills and thrills. I did it to tell the truth. It really sucks being judged by people who have never met you and question your credibility and motivations every step of the way."

Yet questioning Elizondo's credentials is ongoing. According to one investigator, "There is no discernible evidence that he ever worked for a government UFO program, must less led one." And the program he claimed to be in charge of? It existed, but a Pentagon spokesperson has gone on record as saying, "Mr. Elizondo had no responsibilities with regard to the AATIP [Advanced Aerospace Threat Identification Program] while he worked in OUSDI [the Office of Under Secretary of Defense for Intelligence], up until he resigned effective 10/4/2017."

So...it appears Elizondo did work for the Department of Defense, but his role there is unclear. Some have now equated him with Richard Doty, a former special agent for the U.S. Air Force Office of Special Investigations, who has admitted he had been part of programs to deliberately spread disinformation among UFO researchers. Considering Doty's admission, it becomes difficult to sort out truth from disinformation from his past statements. Can Doty be trusted? He is an admitted liar. Now Elizondo finds himself painted with the same brush.

What's Next?

What's the next road sign in the UFO truth vs. UFO lies superhighway going to be? It's difficult to say. On the one hand, nearly everyone is walking around with a camera and recording device in their pocket. On the other hand, photo imaging software like Photoshop exist. Most phones come with some kind of video editing software that can do at least some basic things. How can we tell which photos and videos are real (even if they are real misidentifications), and which are hoaxes?

Then there are the deliberate disinformation campaigns we know have been perpetuated by the military. Can military, and ex-military, witnesses be trusted? One would like to think so, but the question is still very relevant.

The "Roswelling" of sightings continues for those who like to keep the stories going, or who like to embellish them, so that it becomes difficult, after a time, to distinguish what actually happened from what has been added to the legend in the years since the original sighting.

Also, it stretches credulity to think that so many people, from so many governments, and so many governmental agencies, over so many decades, have been so adept at keeping the secret of alien contact. *No one* has been able to come forward with good evidence? Consider how poorly these agencies keep people silent, apparently even after threats against them. Very little, if anything, seems to have slowed the spigot gushing out videos on YouTube, Amazon Prime, and other places online. Is no one in one of these secret government agencies noticing how poorly their secrets are being kept?

The obvious answer is, there's nothing to see here, and a million YouTube videos on alien contact only serve to keep people distracted from whatever the government actually wishes to keep secret. Perhaps it's the next generation of stealth technology, or a new artificial intelligence that can do more than beat a grand master at chess. I have no idea, but if UFOs turn out to be a distraction rather than an actual phenomenon, the agencies in charge of those secrets will have done a very good job indeed.

Into the Night

There's a fascinating frailty of the human mind that psychologists know all about, called "argument from ignorance." This is how it goes. You see lights flashing in the sky. You've never seen anything like this before and don't understand what it is. You say, "It's a UFO!" But then you say, "I don't know what it is; it must be aliens from outer space, visiting from another planet." The issue here is that if you don't know what something is, your interpretation of it should stop immediately. You don't then say it must be X or Y or Z. That's argument from ignorance. I'm not blaming anybody; it may relate to our burning need to manufacture answers because we feel uncomfortable about being steeped in ignorance.
Neil deGrasse Tyson, Astronomer

Don't you believe in flying saucers, they ask me? Don't you believe in telepathy?—in ancient astronauts?—in the Bermuda triangle?—in life after death? No, I reply. One person recently, goaded into desperation by the litany of unrelieved negation, burst out, "Don't you believe in anything?" "Yes," I said. "I believe in evidence. I believe in observation, measurement, and reasoning, confirmed by independent observers. I'll believe anything, no matter how wild and ridiculous, if there is evidence for it. The wilder and more ridiculous something is, however, the firmer and more solid the evidence will have to be."
Isaac Asimov, Author

⁎⁎

A Bit of a Downer

I admit that when I started this book, and when I originally decided to write Escaping Normal as a series, I was hoping to find some new evidence to sink my teeth into. As a teenager, I couldn't read enough about the paranormal, and even today, I don't seem to be able to get my fill of YouTube videos purporting to have "scary" ghost footage (it never is, though), or "best evidence yet photographed" of something paranormal (it isn't).

But I keep watching. And now I've got a new pile of books on my desk with all the latest on the Anunnaki, shadow people, and Bigfoot. I can't wait to read it all.

Still, I remain unconvinced. Which is one reason I hope, if you have a story you're willing to tell, you will share it with me, which you can do via Google Forms or email (contact info in the About the Author section).

So, I was hoping to get swept away by something new, something convincing, and I was not.

I have learned some intriguing things, however. Here are a few:

UFOs and the Like are Never *Not* Interesting

I'd wondered for years why the Men in Black actually existed. I mean, they make for a dramatic story—a UFO witness is ready to come forward when suddenly, they are cowed by mysterious agents of...some agency! But that just doesn't make sense, does it?

It would seem to me that the best way to get people to not believe in alien craft would be to ignore the entire thing. Why send agents to threaten someone, thus proving *something exists which actually needs to be covered up!* Your choices are to let ol' Crazy Dave tell his UFO story at the local bar for the one thousandth time, and for the thousandth time, people will laugh at him, or you can show up and give credence to Dave's story. Someone has come to shut him up, after all. And maybe even threatened him or his family!

That makes no sense, unless the Men in Black are threatening ol' Dave about something which never occurred or which has no objective reality. In this instance, the Bennewitz case makes my point. Who knows what the Air Force wanted to keep secret at Kirtland? It's a sure bet Bennewitz, and anyone he spoke with, would never find out as long as the Air Force strung Bennewitz along with ideas of aliens. Disinformation at its finest, though it's a bit of a puzzle to me as to how Bennewitz even arrived at the idea of aliens to begin with. If you live across the street from an Air Force base, and you pick up some odd transmissions on your radio and see weird lights in the sky, wouldn't your first thought be, *it's the Air Force*. Why did Bennewitz hop over the obvious conclusion to get straight to *I've got to warn the Air Force they're being observed by aliens*?

I'm also intrigued by how ineffective the Men in Black are. They threaten people who then tell everyone they've been threatened. The story may not come out for a few years, but still, we wouldn't know about the Men in Black if the people they threaten actually kept their mouths shut.

The Men in Black, or their bosses, are also singularly incapable of taking down some YouTube videos. Shows like *UFO Hunters* routinely find people who think "the government" doesn't want them to talk, and yet, they not only talk, they are recorded, and their interview goes up on the internet for the entire planet to watch.

But as unsuccessful as the Men in Black, or their bosses, are at keeping people quiet, but do seem to be able to keep Congress uninterested.

Stephen Bassett, a lobbyist who founded the Paradigm Research Group, has been attempting for years to get Congress to hold hearings about UFOs. He feels the aliens have been here since at least 1947, and we need Congress to become involved, because "the presence of extraterrestrials is the most important truth in the world today with the greatest potential to alter the present course of human affairs—a course badly in need of a new destination."

Bassett is one who thinks there are levels of secrecy that bypass Congress and the president. He believes they are kept ignorant, much like the hapless President Whitmore in *Independence Day*. "Deep within the bowels of this intelligence complex are career people who view senators and presidents as mere transients. They keep them out of the loop if they can." Others feel similarly. The *UFO Hunters* found someone who has created a chart of the *twenty previously unknown levels of top-secret above the level the President of the United States*. That's a lot of layers of secret on top of layers of secret, that exist for...reasons. After all, do you really need twenty extra layers of secrecy? *Twenty?*

Whether extra layers of secrecy truly exist is intriguing as a thought exercise. But meanwhile, back in the halls of Congress, Bassett has been having difficulty in getting anyone to work with him. He and his group are dismissed as "kooky" because to take UFOs seriously is to invite ridicule. After all, the Weekly World News pegged twelve senators as aliens way back in 1994. Congress may be unwilling to attract that kind of attention again.

Carl Jung

No less a personage than Carl Jung had things to say about UFOs, which surprised me. Not sure why it surprised me; surely, people seeing odd lights in the sky would intrigue someone whose theories discuss the collective unconscious.

Jung's term for the UFO phenomenon was *visionary rumor*. This entailed classifying sightings as "admittedly impressive collection of mistaken observations and conclusions into which subjective psychic prefigurations have been projected." People saw what they expected, or wanted, to see, whether they consciously realized that desire or not.

Part of what interested Jung was that sightings were so contradictory. Aliens were "three feet tall and look like human beings," or were "utterly unlike us," or were "giants fifteen feet tall." Their ships sometimes flew toward aircraft sent to pursue them, and, at other times, fled from them. The ships could be as small as streetlights or over 500 feet in diameter. The pilots of these craft were harmless observers concerned about our newly-developed nuclear technology, or they were overtly hostile (Jung notes that the 1945 disappearance of the five planes of Flight 19 over the Bermuda Triangle was being blamed on aliens by UFO researchers such as Donald Keyhoe).

Jung wrote:

But if it is a case of psychological projection, there must be a psychic cause for it. One can hardly suppose that anything of such world-wide incidence as the UFOs legend is purely fortuitous and so insignificant. The many thousands of individual testimonies must have an equally extensive casual basis. When an assertion of this kind is corroborated practically everywhere, we are driven to assume that a corresponding motive must be present everywhere, too. Though visionary rumors may be caused or accompanied by all manner of outward circumstances, they are basically essentially on an omnipresent emotional foundation, in this case a psychological situation common to all mankind. The basis for this kind of rumor is an emotional tension having its cause in a situation of collective distress or danger, or in a vital psychic need.

Jung left himself open, though, to the possibility that UFOs were objectively real, and not just the result of some societal "psychic need." But while he left this possibility open (mainly due to the fact that UFOs occasionally showed up on radar as physical objects), the coincidence of UFO reports flaring up just at a) the moment humans began the space race, and b) the development of terrible weapons of nuclear mass destruction, meant that *something* was likely to show up in the skies. "...Unconscious contents have projected themselves on these inexplicable heavenly phenomena and given them a significance they in no way deserve."

Sadly, Racism is a Thing For...Reasons?
Unfortunately, one of the interesting things that showed up in my research was one of humankind's least noteworthy traits: tribalism, here in the form of flat-out racism. Very disappointing! Of course, any group of people will have its less-than-savory characters, yet sometimes, these individuals were allowed to rise quite high in the ranks of the UFO-researching community.

Early reports from the 1950s contained statements that seemed to implicate Jews in the UFO plot (so the recent threat of "Jewish space lasers" isn't really that new, in a sense—conspiracy theorists have pegged the Jews as being present in space for decades now). Men in Black were routinely described as "dark" or "swarthy." Witnesses who tried pinning an ethnicity onto the Men in Black variously described them as "Italian, Burmese, or Indian."

But even if we dismiss some of this as language that would have been more acceptable in the 1950s, there's still the much more recent flak that

MUFON has been dealing with as the racists within its ranks have been more flagrant in publically sounding out about their personal, ahem, *views*. John Ventre, former state director for MUFON's Pennsylvania chapter, posted the following online:

> *Netflix announced a new anti-white show (Dear White People) that promotes white genocide...I don't find this funny. The last thing blacks want is for white males to organize and that's not too far away! White males are the absolute target of the gov't...The media attacks us constantly...Everything this world is was created by Europeans and Americans.*

I refuse to type out more. You can Google the full tirade for yourself. Though Ventre allegedly apologized, his apology seems to have consisted of more "white males are victims" statements, such as, "I'm feeling like because I'm a 60-year-old white man I'm getting totally unfairly attacked here."

Ventre did resign, but so did a lot of other people. Dr. Chris Cogswell, who had been MUFON's Director of Research, was one of them. He, apparently, knew of Ventre's views and had assumed the organization had booted him. When he found out Ventre was still an active MUFON member, Cogswell resigned. "My internal conscience would not let me continue." His resignation letter reads, in part:

> *It is with a heavy heart that I must report my resignation from my position as director of research for the Mutual UFO Network. Yesterday afternoon (Friday, April 13th, 2018) it came to my attention that John Ventre, former state director for Pennsylvania, has had a continued role within MUFON as an active member, is listed as a paid consultant, conference coordinator, and treasurer for the PA chapter, and is a part of the preparations for the upcoming symposium. I believed, as I am sure the vast majority of the interested public believes, that he had been completely removed from MUFON and any attempt to return to the fold of this organization would have been completely and instantly rebuffed...I am sorry that my trust was misplaced..."*

Though I was a bit taken aback that someone with Ventre's views rose to be a state director of a national organization, I had been, I admit, wondering about the overwhelming whiteness and maleness of the organizations I saw online and on television. To a remarkable degree, and with a few exceptions, most of the UFO hunter, Bigfoot/Sasquatch hunter, ghost hunter, etc., television shows feature white males. Even before I started researching these books, I had begun to mock the phenomenon a bit. Upon watching a new-for-me show, and noticing the cast, I'd call out to my husband, "Oh, look! More middle-aged white dudes!"

Whether this is due to middle-aged white men having the financial wherewithal to wander the country looking for aliens, Bigfoot, thunderbirds, ghosts, or what-have-you, while they leave wives at home with the kids, or if television show executives gravitate toward white men as hosts, or if it is that conspiracy theorists who rise in the ranks of such organizations are generally white and male, I do not know. Perhaps it is all three.

Lastly, I noticed, while thumbing through my new copy of Craig Campobasso's *The Extraterrestrial Species Almanac*, that aliens seem to be either monstrous (reptilians), short and weird-looking servile races (grays), or appear white (though sometimes the description says the race comes in many skin colors, the illustrations look overwhelmingly European). I'm not the first to notice this trend, as the term "Nordics" has been applied to the aliens which look more like us. Or, more like *some* of us, that is.

I have a feeling that delving into this issue would require a book of its own, so I will leave the topic here. I will, in fairness to what I hope is the vast majority of MUFON's members, finish by quoting a non-white attendee at a MUFON chapter meeting shortly after the Ventre debacle. "I left pleasantly surprised at the camaraderie I found. It felt almost spiritual. I wanted to return to my father to introduce him to a space that he has only known digitally but that proved more welcoming than I expected."

May that continue to be true.

Come Back For More

Despite not finding what I was looking for in UFO reports, I plan to continue this series. There is just too much about the world that is interesting and weird, even if it turns out to be various manifestations of human psychology.

Assuming I find people willing to share more UFO stories, there may even be a *Descending Skies* 2. But for now, it's off to other destinations—join me as I explore tales of abductions, wild men, flying creatures, demons, fairies, and more. Some of the roads are dark, some not so much, but they all smell of enigma and mystery. I invite you to wander off into the night along with me, and see where we end up.

Maybe it will be on a spaceship. Who knows?

Works Consulted for the Escaping Normal Series

--, Kate. Personal interview. 12 February 2021.

--, Laura. Personal interview. 16 February 2021.

"1561 Celestial Phenomenon Over Nuremberg," Wikipedia. en.wikipedia.org/wiki/1561_celestial_phenomenon_over_Nuremberg, accessed 9 Mar 2021.

"The Alaska Triangle: Unexplained Disappearances." YouTube. Uploaded by Top Mysteries, 17 Jan 2020, www.youtube.com/watch?v=nLb6tMDqiJw, accessed 9 Mar 2021.

Allen, Lauretta. Personal interview. 6 February 2021.

"Are the Mysterious Dogu Figurines Depictions of Alien Astronauts?" Ancient-Code.com, no upload date given, www.ancient-code.com/are-the-mysterious-dogu-figurines-depictions-of-ancient-astronauts/, accessed 12 Apr 2021.

Arkowitz, Hal and Scott O. Lilienfield. "Why Science Tells Us Not to Rely on Eyewitness Accounts." Scientific American. Uploaded 1 Jan 2010. www.scientificamerican.com/article/do-the-eyes-have-it/, accessed 11 Mar 2021.

Berry, Richard B., MD. "Parasomnias." Science Direct. 2012. www.sciencedirect.com/topics/medicine-and-dentistry/hypnopompic, accessed 16 Apr 2021.

Billings, Lee. "Astronomer Avi Loeb Says Aliens Have Visited, and He's Not Kidding." Scientific American, 1 Feb 2021, www.scientificamerican.com/article/astronomer-avi-loeb-says-aliens-have-visited-and-hes-not-kidding1/, accessed 17 Mar 2021.

Bowers, Kenneth S., and John D. Eastwood. "On the Edge of Science: Coping With UFOlogy Scientifically." *Psychological Inquiry*, vol. 7, no. 2, Apr. 1996, p. 136.

Boyle, Rebecca. "The Milky Way is Disappearing." theatlantic.com, uploaded 10 Jun 2016, www.theatlantic.com/science/archive/2016/06/pawnee-sky/486557/, accessed 21 Mar 2021.

"The Bridgewater Triangle." Amazon Prime. www.amazon.com/Bridgewater-Triangle-Loren-Coleman/dp/B01LXMVMI, accessed 6 Mar 2021.

Brookesmith, Peter. *UFO: The Complete Sightings.* New York: Barnes & Noble, 1995.

Campobasso, Craig. *The Extraterrestrial Species Almanac: The Ultimate Guide to Greys, Reptilians, Hybrids, and Nordics.* Massachusetts: Red Wheel, 2021.

"The Celestial Bodies to Blame for Many UFO Sightings." YouTube. Uploaded by Smithsonian Channel, 4 Dec 2015, www.youtube.com/watch?v=KGawp7wBogk, accessed 9 Mar 2021.

Chabris, Christopher and Daniel Simons. "The Invisible Gorilla." theinvisiblegorilla.com, uploaded 2010, www.theinvisiblegorilla.com/gorilla_experiment.html, accessed 11 Mar 2021.

Chew, Stephen L. "Myth: Eyewitness Testimony is the Best Kind of Evidence." *Association for Psychological Science*, uploaded 20 Aug 2018, www.psychologicalscience.org/teaching/myth-eyewitness-testimony-is-the-best-kind-of-evidence.html, accessed 11 Mar 2021.

Choi, Charles Q. "'Alien Megastructure Star May Not Be So Special After All." Space.com, uploaded 19 Sep 2019. www.space.com/alien-megastructure-mysteriously-dimming-stars.html, accessed 16 Mar 2021.

Clancy, Susan A. *Abducted: How People Come to Believe They Were Kidnapped by Aliens*. Massachusetts: Harvard University Press, 2005.

Clark, Steven E., and Elizabeth F. Loftus. "The Construction of Space Alien Abduction Memories." Psychological Inquiry, vol. 7, no. 2, Apr. 1996, p. 140.

Clarke, Ardy Sixkiller. *Space Age Indians: Their Encounters with the Blue Men, Reptilians, and Other Star People*. Texas: Anomalist Books, 2019.

Clarke, David. "Radar Angels." *Fortean Times* 195 (2005), no upload date given, drdavidclarke.co.uk/radar-uaps/radar-angels/, accessed 17 Mar 2021.

Cookney, Francesca. "AMMACH: Britain's weirdest support group says 1,500 people are abducted by aliens each year." Mirror, 9 June 2013, www.mirror.co.uk/news/weird-news/ammach-britains-weirdest-support-group-194040, accessed 28 Apr 2021.

Cromie, William J. "Alien abduction claims examined: signs of trauma found." The Harvard Gazette, uploaded 20 Feb 2003, news.harvard.edu/gazette/story/2003/02/alien-abduction-claims-examined-2/, accessed 5 April 2021.

Curry, Eugene A. "The Final (Missions) Frontier: Extraterrestrials, Evangelism, and the Wide Circle of Human Empathy." *Zygon: Journal of Religion & Science*, vol. 54, no. 3, Sept. 2019, pp. 588–601.

Daugherty, Greg. "Meet J. Allen Hynek, the Astronomer Who First Classified UFO 'Close Encounters.'" History.com Updated 15 Jan 2020. www.history.com/news/j-allen-hynek-ufos-project-blue-book, accessed 10 Mar 2021.

Daugherty, Greg and Missy Sullivan. "Huge, Hovering and Silent: The Mystery of 'Black Triangle' UFOs." history.com, 22 Jul 2020, www.history.com/news/black-triangle-ufos-facts, accessed 18, Mar 2021.

DeGrazier, Michael, director. "Missing 411: The Hunted." Amazon Prime. 2019. www.amazon.com/gp/video/detail/B08B3CNH4C/ref=atv_dl_rdr?autopla y=1, accessed 14 Apr 2021.

Dewan, William J. "'A Saucerful of Secrets': An Interdisciplinary Analysis of UFO Experiences." *Journal of American Folklore,* vol. 119, no. 472, Spring 2006, pp. 184–202.

Dolan, Richard. *The Alien Agendas: A Speculative Analysis of Those Visiting Earth.* New York: Richard Dolan Press, 2020.

Draper, Scott, and Joseph O. Baker. "Angelic Belief as American Folk Religion." *Sociological Forum,* vol. 26, no. 3, Sept. 2011, pp. 623–643

Eby, Sharon. *Bigfoot Beyond Belief: A Study in Cultural Anthropology of What People Believe About Bigfoot/Sasquatch.* Nova Scotia: Sharon Eby, 2021.

Eghigian, Greg. "How UFO Reports Change with the Technology of the Times." Smithsonianmag.com, uploaded 1 Feb 2018, www.smithsonianmag.com/history/how-ufo-reports-change-with-technology-times-180968011/, accessed 18 Mar 2021.

"Extraterrestrial Highway." TravelNevada. travelnevada.com/road-trip/extraterrestrial-highway/, accessed 5 Mar 2021.

"Europa Clipper." NASA.gov, no upload date given. europa.nasa.gov/europa/life-ingredients/, accessed 17 Mar 2021.

Finkelstein, Joshua D. "The Ψ-Files: A Review of the Psychological Literature Regarding False Memories of Alien Abduction." *New School Psychology Bulletin,* vol. 14, no. 1, Jan. 2017, pp. 37–44.

Garber, Megan. "The Man Who Introduced the World to Flying Sarucers: Kenneth Arnold saw something, said something, and ushered in the UFO-industrial complex." The Atlantic. 15 Jun 2014. www.theatlantic.com/technology/archive/2014/06/the-man-who-introduced-the-world-to-flying-saucers/372732/, accessed 9 Mar 2021.

Gault, Matthew. "Researchers Think They Solved the Mystery of America's 'Lost Colony.'" Vice. 18 Aug 2020, www.vice.com/en/article/4aypdq/lost-colony-of-roanoke-mystery-solved-new-book-claims, accessed 30 Mar 2021.

Geiger, John. *The Third Man Factor: Surviving the Impossible.* New York: Weinstein Books, 2009.

Gentile, A.J. "The Nevada Triangle | 2,000 Planes Mysteriously Crashed & Missing Near Area 51." YouTube. Uploaded by The Why Files, 21 January 2021, www.youtube.com/watch?v=WMETBHvo-U4

Gilhus, Ingvile Sælid, Alexandros Tsakos, Marta Camilla Wright, eds. *The Archangel Michael in Africa: History, Cult, and Persona*. London: Bloomsbury Academic, 2021.

Godawa, Brian. *When Giants Were Upon the Earth: The Watchers, the Nephilim, and the Biblical Cosmic War of the Seed*. New York: Warrior Poet Publishing, 2021.

Grande, Todd. "Alien Abduction Story Analysis | Travis Walton/Joe Rogan Interview." YouTube. Dr. Todd Grande, uploaded 4 Feb 2021, www.youtube.com/watch?v=NB0RA6dnYKs, accessed 7 Apr 2021.

Green, Joseph P., et al. "Hypnosis and Psychotherapy: From Mesmer to Mindfulness." *Psychology of Consciousness: Theory, Research, and Practice*, vol. 1, no. 2, June 2014, pp. 199–212.

Green, Joseph P., et al. "Hypnotic Pseudomemories, Prehypnotic Warnings, and the Malleability of Suggested Memories." *Applied Cognitive Psychology*, vol. 12, no. 5, Oct. 1998, pp. 431–444.

Grush, Loren. "NASA is updating its guidelines on how to prevent contamination of the Solar System," theverge, uploaded 9 Jul 2020, www.theverge.com/2020/7/9/21318986/nasa-planetary-protection-guidelines-moon-mars-artemis-human-exploration, accessed 17 Mar 2021.

Hall, William J. and Jimmy Petonito. *Phantom Messages: Chilling Phone Calls, Letters, Emails, and Texts from Unknown Callers*. Massachusetts: Disinformation Books, 2018.

Harpur, Patrick. *Daimonic Reality: A Field Guide to the Otherworld*. Washington: Pine Winds Press, 1994.

Heaney, Christopher. "The Racism Behind Alien Mummy Hoaxes: Pre-Columbian bodies are once again being usd as evidence for extraterrestrial life." The Atlantic. Uploaded 1 Aug 2017, www.theatlantic.com/science/archive/2017/08/how-to-fake-an-alien-mummy/535251/, accessed 12 Apr 2021.

Hollars, B. J. "In Defense of Sasquatch." *Ninth Letter*, vol. 8, no. 1, Spring/Summer 2011, pp. 59–66.

Horselenberg, Robert, et al. "Individual Differences in the Accuracy of Autobiographical Memory." *Clinical Psychology & Psychotherapy*, vol. 11, no. 3, May 2004, pp. 168–176.

"How Color Affects Taste: A Lesson in Gastrophysics." Food Republic, uploaded 29 Jun 2017. medium.com/@foodrepublic/how-color-affects-taste-a-lesson-in-gastrophysics-1c1d3df89702, accessed 12 Mar 2021.

"I Was Abducted by Aliens." YouTube. Uploaded by Truly, 17 Jan 2021, www.youtube.com/watch?v=IU6UPMTKazY, accessed 31 Jan 2021.

"Indrid Cold – Casefiles #1." YouTube. Small Town Monsters, uploaded 1 Nov 2017. www.youtube.com/watch?v=_0JfU3ch-AY, accessed 22 Mar 2021.

Irwin, Neil. "For New UFO Lobby, 'X-Files' Are Real." Christian Science Monitor, vol. 91, no. 183, 17 Aug. 1999, p. 5. EBSCOhost, search.ebscohost.com/login.aspx?direct=true&db=aph&AN=2159350&site =ehost-live&scope=site.

Janssen, Volker. "How the 'Little Green Men' Phenomenon Began on a Kentucky Farm." History.com, uploaded 2 Jan 2020. www.history.com/news/little-green-men-origins-aliens-hopkinsville, accessed 6 Apr 2021.

Johanson, Donald and Maitland Edey. Lucy: The Beginnings of Humankind. New York: Warner Books, 1981.

Jung, C. G. "A Visionary Rumour." Journal of Analytical Psychology, vol. 4, no. 1, Jan. 1959, pp. 5–19.

Keel, John A. The Complete Guide to Mysterious Beings. New York: Doubleday, 1970.

Kelley-Romano, Stephanie. "Mythmaking in Alien Abduction Narratives." Communication Quarterly, vol. 54, no. 3, Aug. 2006, pp. 383–406.

Kiessling, Nicolas K. "Grendel: A New Aspect." Modern Philology, vol. 65, no. 3, Feb 1968, pp. 191-201.

Kloor, Keith. "The Media Loves This UFO Expert Who Says He Worked for an Obscure Pentagon Program. Did he?" The Intercept. Uploaded 1 Jun 2019, theintercept.com/2019/06/01/ufo-unidentified-history-channel-luis-elizondo-pentagon/, accessed 25 Mar 2021.

Kloor, Keith. "UFOs Won't Go Away." Issues in Science & Technology, vol. 35, no. 3, Spring 2019, pp. 49–56.

Lamberg, Lynne. "Belief in Alien UFOs Deep in American Psyche." JAMA, vol. 278, no. 3, July 16, 1997, pp. 193.

Landau, Elizabeth. "What We Know—And Don't Know—About 'Oumuamua." NASA, 27 Jun 2018. solarsystem.nasa.gov/news/473/what-we-knowand-dont-knowabout-oumuamua/, accessed 17 Mar 2021.

"Life on Titan." European Space Agency, no upload date given, esa.int/ Science_Exploration/Space_Science/Cassini-Huygens/Life_on_Titan, accessed 17 Mar 2021.

Lumpkin, Joseph B. The Books of Enoch: The Angels, The Watchers, and the Nephilim. Alabama: Fifth Estate Publishers, 2015.

Lynn, Heather. The Anunnaki Connection: Sumerian Gods, Alien DNA & The Fate of Humanity. Massachusetts: New Page Books, 2020.

Lynn, Heather. Evil Archaeology: Demons, Possessions, and Sinister Relics. Massachusetts: Disinformation Books, 2019.

Lyon, Jason. "To Pay Attention, the Brain Uses Filters, Not a Spotlight." Quanta Magazine. 24 Sep 2019. www.quantamagazine.org/to-pay-attention-the-brain-uses-filters-not-a-spotlight-20190924/, accessed 11 Mar 2021.

Martin, Jean-Rémy, and Elisabeth Pacherie. "Alterations of Agency in Hypnosis: A New Predictive Coding Model." *Psychological Review*, vol. 126, no. 1, Jan. 2019, pp. 133–152.

"The Maury Island Incident." HowStuffWorks, Uploaded by the Editors of Publications International, LTD. science.howstuffworks.com/space/aliens-ufos/maury-island-incident.htm, accessed 9 Mar 2021.

McClenon, James. "A Community Survey of Psychological Symptoms: Evaluating Evolutionary Theories Regarding Shamanism and Schizophrenia." Mental Health, Religion & Culture, vol. 15, no. 8, Oct. 2012, pp. 799–816.

McGaha, James and Joe Nickell. "The Roswellian Syndrome: How Some UFO Myths Develop." Skeptical Inquirer, Volume 36, No. 3, May/June 2012. skepticalinquirer.org/2012/05/the-roswellian-syndrome-how-some-ufo-myths-develop/, accessed 9 Mar 2021.

"McGurk Effect – Auditory Illusion – BBC Horizon Clip." YouTube. Uploaded by sixfullofnines, 16 Mar 2016, www.youtube.com/watch?v=2k8fHR9jKVM

McLachlan, Sean. *Hollow Earth: A History of the Strange Tales, Bizarre Beliefs, and Conspiracy Theories about the Earth's Core*. Illinois: Charles River Editors, 2017.

McRobbie, Linda Rodriguez. "Why alien abductions are down dramatically." Boston Globe. Uploaded 12 Jul 2016. www.bostonglobe.com/ideas/2016/06/11/why-alien-abductions-are-down-dramatically/qQ3zdBIc2tLAf3LVms8GLP/story.html, accessesd 14 Apr 2021.

Meldrum, Jeff. "Sasquatch & Other Wildmen: The Search for Relict Hominoids." *Journal of Scientific Exploration*, vol. 30, no. 3, Fall 2016, pp. 355–373.

Mencken, F.Carson, et al. "Round Trip to Hell in a Flying Saucer: The Relationship between Conventional Christian and Paranormal Beliefs in the United States." *Sociology of Religion*, vol. 70, no. 1, Spring 2009, pp. 65–85.

"Missing 411—Behind the Mysteries: Strange disappearances in national parks." Paranormal Authority, no upload date given, paranormalauthority.com/missing-411/, accessed 30 Mar 2021.

Mobley, Gregory. "The Wild Man in the Bible and the Ancient Near East." *Journal of Biblical Literature*, vol. 116, no. 2, Summer 1997, p. 217.

Morris, Gregory L. "Imagining Bigfoot." *Western American Literature*, vol. 42, no. 3, Fall 2007, pp. 276–292.

Newman, Leonard S., and Roy F. Baumeister. "Toward an Explanation of the UFO Abduction Phenomenon: Hypnotic Elaboration, Extraterrestrial Sadomasochism, and Spurious Memories." *Psychological Inquiry*, vol. 7, no. 2, Apr. 1996, p. 99

Nickell, Joe. "Famous Alien Abduction In Pascagoula: Reinvestigating a Cold Case." Skeptical Inquirer Volume 36, No. 3. skepticalinquirer.org/2012/05/famous-alien-abduction-in-pascagoula-reinvestigating-a-cold-case/, accessed 9 Mar 2021.

Nickell, Joe, Barry Karr and Tom Genomi, editors. *The Outer Edge: Classic Investigations of the Paranormal*. New York: CSICOP, 1996.

Nie, Fanhao, and Daniel V. A. Olson. "Demonic Influence: The Negative Mental Health Effects of Belief in Demons." *Journal for the Scientific Study of Religion*, vol. 55, no. 3, Sept. 2016, pp. 498–515.

Nita, Maria. "Sky vs. Earthly Empowerment: From Angels and Superheroes to Humans and Community in the Marvel Universe and Green Christian Cosmology." *Journal of Religion & Popular Culture*, vol. 31, no. 3, Sept. 2019, pp. 236–249.

Novotney, Amy. "The risks of social isolation." apa.org, uploaded 15 May 2019, Vol 50, No. 5. apa.org/monitor/2019/05/ce-corner-isolation, accessed 17 Mar 2021.

Offutt, Jason. *Darkness Walks: The Shadow People Among Us*. New York: Anomalist Books, 2009.

Orne, Martin T. and A. Gordon Hammer, eds. "Hypnosis." Encyclopaedia Britannica. No upload date given. www.britannica.com/science/hypnosis, accessed 19 Apr 2021.

Patry, Alain L., and Luc G. Pelletier. "Extraterrestrial Beliefs and Experiences: An Application of the Theory of Reasoned Action." *Journal of Social Psychology*, vol. 141, no. 2, Apr. 2001, pp. 199–217.

Petrich, Loren. "Close Encounters of the Various Kinds." lpetrich.org/UFOs/Close%20Encounters.xhtml, accessed 9 Mar 2021.

Phelan, Matthew. "Navy Pilot Who Filmed the 'Tic Tac' UFO Speaks: 'It Wasn't Behaving by the Normal Laws of Physics.'" New York Intelligencer, 19 Dec 2019, nymag.com/intelligencer/2019/12/tic-tac-ufo-video-q-and-a-with-navy-pilot-chad-underwood.html, accessed 18 Mar 2021.

"Problems With Witness Testimony: Tricks Memory Plays." mcadams.posc.mu.edu, No Upload Date Given. mcadams.posc.mu.edu/memory.htm, accessed 11 Mar 2021.

Prothero, Donald. "The Hollow Earth: If You Thought the Flat Earthers Were Out There, Wait Until You Read About Those Who Think the Earth Is an Empty Sphere Filled With Wonders." *Skeptic*, vol. 25, no. 3, July 2020, pp. 18–23.

Pugliese, David. "Journey to Area 51: Black helicopters and claims of abductions by aliens." Ottawa Citizen, uploaded 19 Sept 2019, ottawacitizen.com/news/national/defence-watch/journey-to-area-51-black-helicopters-and-claims-of-alien-abductions, accessed 22 Mar 2021.

Pyle, Robert Michael. *Where Bigfoot Walks: Crossing the Dark Divide.* Berkeley, California: Counterpoint, 1995.

Randle, Kevin D. *The Government UFO Files: The Conspiracy of Cover-Up.* Michigan: Visible Ink Press, 2014.

"Recent Adverse Publicity on Parapsychological Research." CIA.gov. www.cia.gov/readingroom/docs/CIA-RDP96-00788R001100360001-1.pdf, accessed 11 Mar 2021.

Ricksecker, Mike. *A Walk in the Shadows: A Complete Guide to Shadow People, 2nd edition.* USA; Haunted Road Media, 2021.

Robin, Frédérique, et al. "Hypnosis and False Memories." *Psychology of Consciousness: Theory, Research, and Practice*, vol. 5, no. 4, Dec. 2018, pp. 358–373.

Rogo, D. Scott. *The Haunted House Handbook.* Tempo Books: United States, 1978.

Rojas, Alejandro. "New survey shows nearly half of Americans believe in aliens." Huffpost, Uploaded 02 Aug 2017, www.huffpost.com/entry/new-survey-shows-nearly-half-of-americans-believe-in_b_59824c11e4b03d0624b0abe4, accessed 29 Mar 2021.

Rojcewicz, Peter M. "The 'Men in Black' Experience and Tradition: Analogues with the Traditional Devil Hypothesis." The Journal of American Folklore, vol. 100, no. 396, 1987, pp. 148–160. JSTOR, www.jstor.org/stable/540919. Accessed 22 Mar. 2021.

Roos, Dave. "When UFOs Buzzed the White House and the Air Force Blamed the Weather." History. www.history.com/news/ufos-washington-white-house-air-force-coverup, accessed 9 Mar 2021.

Rose, Steve. "The real Men in Black, Hollywood and the great UFO cover-up." theguardian.com, uploaded 14 Aug 2014. www.theguardian.com/film/2014/aug/14/men-in-black-ufo-sightings-mirage-makers-movie, accessed 22 Mar 2021.

Sayers, William. "Middle English 'Wodewose' 'Wilderness Being': A Hybrid Etymology?" *ANQ*, vol. 17, no. 3, Summer 2004, pp. 12–20.

Seemangal, Robin. "Meet the Lobbyist Pressuring the US Gov't to Disclose Extraterrestrial Activity." Observer, uploaded 16 Sep 2015, observer.com/2015/09/meet-the-lobbyist-pressuring-the-us-government-to-disclose-extraterrestrial-activity/, accessed 23 Mar 2021.

Segura, Olga. "True alienation: when a person of color tries to fit in with UFO enthusiasts." theguardian.com, uploaded 6 Mar 2020, www.theguardian.com/world/2020/mar/06/aliens-ufos-olga-segura, accessed 24 Mar 2021.

Seth, Anil. "Your Brain Hallucinates Your Conscious Reality." YouTube. Uploaded by TED, 18 Jul 2017, www.youtube.com/watch?v=lyu7v7nWzfo, Accessed 7 Mar 2021.

Sheaffer, Robert. *The UFO Verdict: Examining the Evidence*. New York: Prometheus Books, 1986.

Shinn, Sharon. Personal Correspondence, 15 Apr 2021.

Shubin, Neil. *Your Inner Fish: A Journey Into the 3.5-Billion-Year History of the Human Body*. New York: Vintage Books, 2009.

Siegel, Ethan. "The 5 Possibilities for Life on Mars." Forbes, Uploaded 4 Aug 2020, www.forbes.com/sites/startswithabang/2020/08/04/the-5-possibilities-for-life-on-mars/?sh=73c24d195387, accessed 17 Mar 2021.

Simon, Edward. "Why Sasquatch and Other Crypto-Beasts Haunt Our Imaginations." *Anthropology of Consciousness*, vol. 28, no. 2, Fall 2017, pp. 117–120.

"Solar System Exploration: Titan," NASA.gov, no upload date given, solarsystem.nasa.gov/moons/saturn-moons/titan/in-depth/, accessed 17 Mar 2021.

Spanos, Nicholas P., and Patricia A. Cross. "Close Encounters: An Examination of UFO Experiences." *Journal of Abnormal Psychology*, vol. 102, no. 4, Nov. 1993, p. 624.

Spitznagel, Eric. "Why hundreds of people vanish into the American wilderness." New York Post, uploaded 4 Jul 2020, nypost.com/2020/07/04/why-hundreds-of-people-vanish-into-the-american-wilderness/, accessed 29 Mar 2021.

Steffen, Andrea D. "Researchers Have Made Self-Assembling DNA Nanobots with Encoded Structural Plans," Intelligent Living, Uploaded 18 Feb 2021, www.intelligentliving.co/self-assembling-dna-nanobots/, accessed 26 Apr 2021.

Stephey, M.J. "A Brief History of UFOs." *Time*. 17 Dec 2009. content.time.com/time/health/article/0,8599,1948214,00.html. Accessed 5 Mar 2021.

Stockton, Steve. *Strange Things In the Woods: A Collection of Terrifying Stories.* Beyond the Fray Publishing, 2013.

Stover, Dawn. "Double Dread: UFOs and Nuclear War." the bulletin.org, 4 Jun 2019, thebulletin.org/2019/06/double-dread-ufos-and-nuclear-war/, accessed 20 Mar 2021.

Sumner, Mark. Personal Correspondence, 9 Apr 2021.

Swami, Viren, et al. "The Truth Is Out There: The Structure of Beliefs About Extraterrestrial Life Among Austrian and British Respondents." *Journal of Social Psychology,* vol. 149, no. 1, Feb. 2009, pp. 29–43.

Swami, Viren, et al. "Psychology in Outerspace: Personality, Individual Difference, and Demographic Predictors of Beliefs about Extraterrestrial Life." *European Psychologist,* vol. 15, no. 3, 2010, pp. 220–228.

Taylor, Timothy. *The Buried Soul: How Humans Invented Death.* Boston: Beacon Press, 2002.

"Terror in the Skies." Amazon Prime, www.amazon.com/Terror-Skies-Thunderbirds-Prehistoric-Remnants/dp/B07RNN1NFK, accessed 6 Mar 2021.

"UFO Hunters: Full Episode-Reverse Engineering (Season 1, Episode 7) | History." YouTube. History.com. 24 Feb 2019, www.youtube.com/watch?v=GokNWVlpius, accessed 11 Mar 2021.

"UFO Hunters: Terrifying Encounters with Mysterious Beings (S3, E12) | Full Episode | History." YouTube. History.com. 8 Mar 2021, www.youtube.com/watch?v=w7z7u6enuNw&t=39s, accessed 9 Mar 2021.

"UFO Sightings Surge Across US | Unidentified (Season 2) | History." YouTube. Uploaded by History, 4 Sep 2020, www.youtube.com/watch?v=y-6rgZwY04g, accessed 9 Mar 2021.

"UFOstalker.com." Accessed 10 Mar 2021.

Unacknowledged. Mike Mazzola. Amazon Prime, 2017.

Vallee, Jacques. *Passport to Magonia: From Folklore to Flying Saucers.* Brisbane, Australia: Daily Grail Publishing, 1969.

Vidyasagar, Aparna. "What is CRISPR?" LiveScience. Uploaed 21 Apr 2018. www.livescience.com/58790-crispr-explained.html, accessed 12 Apr 2021.

Wagstaff, Graham F. "Is There a Future for Investigative Hypnosis?" *Journal of Investigative Psychology & Offender Profiling,* vol. 6, no. 1, Jan. 2009, pp. 43–57.

Wall, Mike. "UFOs Are Real, But Don't Assume They're Alien Spaceships," space.com, 31 May 2019, www.space.com/ufos-real-but-not-alien-spaceships.html, accessed 17 Mar 2021.

Webster, Donovan. "In 1947, A High-Altitude Balloon Crash Landed in Roswell. The Aliens Never Left: Despite its persistence in popular culture, extraterrestrial life owes more to the imagination than reality." *Smithsonian Magazine*, 5 Jul 2017, www.smithsonianmag.com/smithsonian-institution/in-1947-high-altitude-balloon-crash-landed-roswell-aliens-never-left-180963917/, accessed 9 Mar 2021.

Welfare, Simon and John Fairley. *Arthur C. Clarke's Mysterious World*. New York: Trident International Television Enterprises, 1980.

Welsh, Tim. "It feels instantaneous, but how long does it really take to think a thought?" *The Conversation*. 26 June 2015. www.theconversation.com/it-feels-instantaneous-but-how-long-does-it-really-take-to-think-a-thought-42392 Accessed 6 Mar 2021.

Westrum, Ron. "Social Intelligence about Anomalies: The Case of UFOs." Social Studies of Science, vol. 7, no. 3, 1977, pp. 271–302. JSTOR, www.jstor.org/stable/284599, accessed 5 Mar. 2021.

Whalen, Andrew. "Are Aliens Real? One-Third of Americans Think Alien UFOs Have Visited Earth." *Newsweek*, uploaded 6 Sep 2019, www.newsweek.com/aliens-are-real-ufos-2019-sightings-americans-area-51-raid-extraterrestrial-disclosure-1458103, accessed 16 Mar 2021.

Whalen, Andrew. "What if Aliens Met Racists? MUFON Resignations Highlight Internal Divisions in UFO Sightings Organization." *Newsweek*, uploaded 29 Apr 2018, www.newsweek.com/ufo-sightings-mufon-2018-john-ventre-alien-extraterrestrial-905060, accessed 24 Mar 2021.

"What is Nanotechnology?" nano.gov, no upload date given, www.nano.gov/nanotech-101/what/definition, accessed 18 Mar 2021.

"What is Sleep Paralysis?" Sleep Foundation. 6 Aug 2020. www.sleepfoundation.org/parasomnias/sleep-paralysis, accessed 16 Apr 2021.

"Where are memories stored in the brain?" Queensland Brain Institute. Uploaded 23 Jul 2018, qbi.uq.edu.au/brain-basics/memory/where-are-memories-stored#:~:text=The%20hippocampus%2C%20located%20in%20the,with%20a%20friend%20last%20week, accessed 19 Apr 2021.

Wilkins, Jacob. "The Nuremberg UFO Sighting of 1561," *Medium.com*, 18 Nov 2020, medium.com/lessons-from-history/the-nuremberg-ufo-sighting-of-1561-4078ecfcd946, accessed 9 Mar 2021.

Wiseman, Richard. *Paranormality: Why we see what isn't there*. London: MacMillan, 2011.

Witze, Alexandra. "Prospects for Life on Venus Fade—But Aren't Dead Yet." *Nature*, uploaded 17 Nov 2020. www.nature.com/articles/d41586-020-03258-5, accessed 17 Mar 2021.

Woody, Erik, and Pamela Sadler. "Interpersonal Aspects of Hypnosis: Twisted Pears and Other Forbidden Fruit." *Psychology of Consciousness: Theory, Research, and Practice*, Apr. 2020.

Index

About the Author

Marella Sands is a native St. Louisan who has published novels, novellas, short stories, a poem, an essay, and non-fiction works. Her historical novels, *Sky Knife* and *Serpent and Storm*, were set in 5th century Central America. In addition, she co-wrote two King's Quest novels with fellow St. Louisan Mark Sumner under the name Kenyon Morr. She has had short stories in several anthologies. She has a series set in an alternate United States, which is published by Ring of Fire Press. She also writes the Angels' Share books. She and her husband travel whenever they can. Marella earned degrees in anthropology from the University of Tulsa and Kent State University. The author's household includes the author, her husband, and a multitude of pets.

Word Posse Fun Fact

I've always loved stories of the unusual. Freak storms where frogs rained from the sky? UFOs over Ohio? Aliens and Men in Black wandering about the country? The Mothman of Point Pleasant? Ghosts in old castles? Strange shadows in the basement? Something big and hairy creeping through your campsite? I was hooked on it all. If it were weird, I was reading about it, whether it was Carl Sagan's *The Demon-Haunted World*, John Keel's *The Complete Guide to Mysterious Beings*, or Erich von Däniken's *Chariots of the Gods*. On television, I watched *Project U.F.O.* and *In Search Of*. Needless to say, when *The X*-Files landed on TV, I was there. While I didn't grow up to be a believer in the paranormal, I'm never *not* fascinated with the tales. I hope, with this series, to discuss possible explanations for various phenomena, as well as provide a forum for people to tell their stories. If you have a story you'd like to share, contact me at msands@marellasands.com. Or fill in my Google form at: https://tinyurl.com/eej3wt8 Or go to my website (www.writnfool.com) and click on the link on the right that says "My Paranormal Story." Thanks!